D0211388

INDIAN INK

INDIAN INK
TOM STOPPARD

faber and faber
LONDON · BOSTON

First published in 1995
by Faber and Faber Limited
3 Queen Square London WCIN 3AU
Reprinted with corrections 1995

Photoset by Parker Typesetting Service, Leicester
Printed in England by Clays Ltd, St Ives plc

A CIP record for this book is available
from the British Library

ISBN 0-571-17555-4 (cased)
0-571-17556-2 (pbk)

Indian Ink is dedicated to the memory
of Laura Kendal

CHARACTERS

FLORA CREWE
COOMARASWAMI
NAZRUL
ELEANOR SWAN
ELDON PIKE
ANISH DAS
NIRAD DAS
DAVID DURANCE
DILIP
RESIDENT
ENGLISHWOMAN
ENGLISHMAN
RAJAH/POLITICIAN
NELL
ERIC

In addition:
Indian QUESTIONER(S)
Club SERVANT(S)
Rajah's SERVANT(S)

The play is set in two periods, 1930 (in India) and mid-1980s (in England and India).

It is not intended that the stage be demarcated between India and England, or past and present. Floor space, and even furniture, may be common. In this respect and in others, the play profited greatly from Peter Wood's direction. The stage directions generally follow the original production but are not offered as a blueprint for the staging.

T.S.

Indian Ink had its first performance at the Yvonne Arnaud
Theatre, Guildford, and opened at the Aldwych Theatre,
London, on 27 February 1995, when the cast was as follows:

FLORA CREWE	Felicity Kendal
COOMARASWAMI	Rashid Karapiet
NAZRUL	Ravi Aujla
ELEANOR SWAN	Margaret Tyzack
ELDON PIKE	Colin Stinton
QUESTIONER	Akbar Kurtha
NIRAD DAS	Art Malik
ANISH DAS	Paul Bhattacharjee
DAVID DURANCE	Dominic Jephcott
DILIP	Akbar Kurtha
ENGLISHMAN	Kenneth Jay
ENGLISHWOMAN	Diana Oxford
RESIDENT	Peter Wickham
CLUB SERVANT	Ravi Aujla
RAJAH/POLITICIAN	Madhav Sharma
RAJAH'S SERVANT	Naim Khan-Turk
NELL	Nickie Rainsford
ERIC	Daniel Wellon
Produced by	Michael Codron
Directed by	Peter Wood
Designed by	Carl Toms
Lighting by	Mark Henderson

ACT ONE

Dusk. FLORA *sits alone on a moving train. Her suitcase is on the rack above her head. The train is approaching a station.* FLORA, *already speaking, stands to lift down her suitcase. By the end of her first speech, she is on the station platform at Jummapur.*

FLORA: 'Jummapur, Wednesday, April the second. Darling
    Nell, I arrived here on Saturday from Bombay after a day
    and a night and a day in a Ladies Only, stopping now and
    again to be revictualled through the window with pots of tea
    and proper meals on matinee trays, which, remarkably, you
    hand back through the window at the next station down the
    line where they do the washing up; and from the last stop I
    had the compartment to myself, with the lights coming on
    for me to make my entrance on the platform at Jummapur.
    The President of the Theosophical Society was waiting with
    several members of the committee drawn up at a respectful
    distance, not quite a red carpet and brass band but garlands
    of marigolds at the ready, and I thought there must be
    somebody important on the train – '

COOMARASWAMI: (*Interrupting*) Miss Crewe!

FLORA: '– and it turned out to be me.'

COOMARASWAMI: Welcome to Jummapur!

FLORA: – 'which was very agreeable.' Thank you!
    (*And as she is garlanded by* COOMARASWAMI:)
    How nice! Are you Mr Coomar . . .

COOMARASWAMI: Coomaraswami! That is me! Is this your only
    luggage?! Leave it there!
    (*He claps his hands imperiously for assistance, and then shakes
    hands enthusiastically with* FLORA.)
    How do you *do*, Miss *Crewe*!
    (*The handshake which begins on the station platform ends on
    the verandah of the 'Dak Bungalow', or guesthouse. The
    guesthouse requires a verandah and an interior which includes,
    or comprises, a bedroom. On the verandah is a small table with*

at least two chairs. There is an electric light, unlit, and an oil lamp, lit. The bedroom contains a bed under a mosquito net, a washstand, a bedside table, an electric fan and a 'punkah'. There is a door to a bathroom off-stage.

A servant, NAZRUL, carries Flora's suitcase into the bedroom, and then retreats to his quarters, out of sight.)

FLORA: (Completing the handshake) Thank you!

COOMARASWAMI: Welcome, my dear Miss Crewe! And farewell! A day of rest!

FLORA: Thank you – you were so kind to . . .

COOMARASWAMI: I will leave you! Tomorrow, a picnic! Do you like temples?

FLORA: Well, I don't know . . . I'm sure I . . .

COOMARASWAMI: Leave everything to me!

(COOMARASWAMI leaves her, shouting in Hindi for his buggy-driver.

The Shepperton garden is now visible. Here, MRS SWAN and PIKE are having tea while occupied with a shoebox of Flora's letters.)

FLORA: 'And in no time at all I was installed in a little house, two good-sized rooms under a tin roof . . . with electric light . . . (She tries the electric light switch without result.) . . . and an oil lamp just in case . . .'
(She looks out from the verandah.) '. . . a verandah looking out at a rather hopeless garden . . . but with a good table and chair which does very well for working . . .'
(She tries out the chair and the table.) '. . . and a wicker sofa of sorts for not working . . . and round the back . . .'
(She disappears around the corner of the verandah where it goes out of sight, while MRS SWAN turns a page of the letter.)

MRS SWAN: I wish I'd kept the envelopes, they'd be worth something now, surely, the Indian ones at least.

PIKE: Oh, but it's the wine, not the bottles! These letters are a treasure. They may be the only *family* letters anywhere.

MRS SWAN: I dare say, since I'm the only family.

PIKE: Her handwriting sometimes . . . (He passes a letter to her for assistance.)

MRS SWAN: (Deciphering where he indicates) '. . . a kitchen bit with a refrigerator . . .'

FLORA: (*Reappearing*) '. . . a kitchen bit with a *refrigerator*! But Nazrul, my cook and bottle-washer, disdains the electric stove and makes his own arrangements on a little verandah of his own.'
(*She goes into the interior, into the bedroom, where she tries the switch for the electric fan, again without result.*)
'My bedroom, apart from the electric fan, also has a punkah which is like a pelmet worked by a punkah-wallah who sits outside and flaps the thing by a system of ropes and pulleys, or would if he were here, which he isn't. And then off the bedroom . . .'
(*She disappears briefly through a door.*
MRS SWAN *passes the page to* PIKE *and they continue to read in silence.*)
(*Reappearing*) '. . . is a dressing room and bathroom combined, with a tin tub, and a shower with a head as big as a sunflower – a rainflower, of course . . .'
(PIKE *grunts approvingly*)
'. . . and all this is under a big green tree with monkeys and parrots in the branches, and it's called a duck bungalow . . .'
MRS SWAN: *Dak* bungalow.
FLORA: '. . . although there is not a duck to be seen.'
(*She disappears into the bathroom with her suitcase.*)
MRS SWAN: Dak was the post; they were post-houses, when letters went by runner.
PIKE: Ah . . .
MRS SWAN: I like to have two kinds of cake on the go. The Madeira is my own.
PIKE: I'm really not hungry.
MRS SWAN: I wouldn't let that stop you, Mr Pike, if you hope to get on my good side.
PIKE: I would love some. The Madeira. (*She cuts him a slice.*) And won't you please call me Eldon? (*He takes the slice of cake.*) Thank you. (*He takes the bite and gives a considered verdict.*) Wonderful.
MRS SWAN: I should think so.
PIKE: It's the excitement. There's nothing like these in the British Library, you know!

3

MRS SWAN: (*Amused*) The British Library!

PIKE: The University of Texas has Flora Crewe indexed across twenty-two separate collections! And I still have the Bibliothèque Nationale next week. The *Collected Letters* are going to be a year of my life!

MRS SWAN: A whole year just to collect them?

PIKE: (*Gaily*) The notes, the notes! The notes is where the fun is! You can't just *collect* Flora Crewe's letters into a book and call it 'The Collected Letters of Flora Crewe'. The correspondence of well-known writers is mostly written without a thought for the general reader. I mean, they don't do their own footnotes. So there's an opportunity here. Which you might call a sacred trust. Edited by E. Cooper Pike. There isn't a page which doesn't need – look – you see here? – 'I had a funny dream last night about the Queen's Elm.' Which Queen? What elm? Why was she dreaming about a *tree*? So this is where I come in, wearing my editor's hat. To lighten the darkness.

MRS SWAN: It's a pub in the Fulham Road.

PIKE: Thank you. This is why God made poets and novelists, so the rest of us can get published. Would that be a *chocolate* cake?

MRS SWAN: Why, would you . . .?

PIKE: No, I just thought: did your sister like chocolate cake particularly?

MRS SWAN: What an odd thing to think. Flora didn't like chocolate in any form.

PIKE: Ah. That's interesting. May I?

(PIKE *takes the next page of the letter from the tea-table.*
FLORA *approaches, accompanied by* COOMARASWAMI, *who has a yellow parasol.*)

FLORA: 'The sightseeing with picnic was something of a Progress with the president of the Theosophical Society holding a yellow parasol over me while the committee bicycled alongside, sometimes two to a bike, and children ran before and behind – I felt like a carnival float representing Empire – or, depending how you look at it, the Subjugation of the Indian People, and of course you're right, darling, but I never saw anyone less subjugated than Mr Coomaraswami.'

4

COOMARASWAMI: We have better temples in the south. I am from the south. You are right to be discriminating!

FLORA: (*Apologetically*) Did I seem discriminating? I'm sure it wasn't their fault. The insides of churches . . .

COOMARASWAMI: I understand you completely, Miss Crewe!

FLORA: But I don't know what I'm trying to say!

COOMARASWAMI: That is not a requirement.

FLORA: I'm afraid I'm without religion, you see.

COOMARASWAMI: I *do* see! Which religion are you afraid you are most without?

FLORA: Now, Mr Coomaraswami, turning a phrase may do for Bloomsbury but I expect better from *you*.

'And I told him about Herbert's lady decorator being asked on her deathbed what was her religion and telling the priest, "I'm afraid I worship mauve".'

COOMARASWAMI: (*Thoughtfully*) For me, it is grey.

FLORA: 'I'm going to like India.'

PIKE: (*With letter*) Who was Herbert?

MRS SWAN: Wells.

PIKE: Ah. (*Catching on*) H. G. Wells? Really? (*Cautiously*) You don't mean he and Flora . . .?

MRS SWAN: You should see your face. Flora met him not long before she went out.

PIKE: Out?

MRS SWAN: To India. It must have been round Christmas or New Year. I think I got a postcard from Paris (*She delves into the shoebox.*) Flora loved Paris. Here, look . . . is that it?

PIKE: Paris, yes . . . no, 1924 . . . it's a souvenir of the Olympic Games.

MRS SWAN: Oh yes, the hurdler. Flora apologized publicly in the Chelsea Arts Club. No medals for us in the *hurdles*.

PIKE: Is that *true*, Eleanor?

MRS SWAN: Now, Eldon, you are *not* allowed to write a book, not if you were to eat the entire cake. The *Collected Poems* was a lovely surprise and I'm sure the *Collected Letters* will be splendid, but *biography* is the worst possible excuse for getting people wrong.

FLORA: 'So far, India likes me. My lecture drew a packed house,

5

Mr C's house, in fact, and a much more sensible house than mine, built round a courtyard with a flat roof all round so I had an audience in the gods like gods in the audience . . .'

(*There is the sound of the applause.* COOMARASWAMI *faces the audience with* FLORA. *It is night. There may be a microphone for the public statements.*)

'. . . and it all went terribly well, until . . .'

COOMARASWAMI: Miss Crewe in her wisdom and beauty has agreed to answer questions!

FLORA: ' – and the very first one went – '

QUESTIONER: Miss Crewe, it is said you are an intimate friend of Mr H. G. Wells –

FLORA: ' – and I thought, "God, how unfair! – to have come all this way to be gossiped about as if one were still in the Queen's Elm" – '

PIKE: A public house in the Fulham area of Chelsea.

FLORA: ' – but it turned out nothing was meant by it except – '

QUESTIONER: Does Mr Wells write his famous books with a typewriter or with pen and ink?

FLORA: (*Firmly*) With pen and ink, a Waterman fountain pen, a present from his wife.

(*There is an appreciative hubbub.*)

'Not that I had the least idea – Herbert showed small inclination to write his famous books while I was around.'

PIKE: FC had met Wells no earlier than December and the affair was therefore brief, possibly the weekend of January 7th and 8th; which she spent in Paris.

FLORA: 'After which there was a reception with lemonade and Indian Scotch . . .'

(FLORA *and* COOMARASWAMI *are offered drinks from a tray of drinks. They are joined in due course by the* QUESTIONER.)

'. . . and delicious snacks and conversation – darling, it's so moving, they read the *New Statesman* and the *TLS* as if they were the Bible in parts, well, I don't mean the *Bible* but you know what I mean, and they know who wrote what about whom; it's like children with their faces jammed to the railings of an unattainable park. They ask me – '

QUESTIONER: What is your opinion of Gertrude Stein, Miss Crewe?

FLORA: Oh . . . yes, Gertrude Stein!

'– and I can't bring myself to say she's a poisonous old baggage who's travelling on a platform ticket . . .'

PIKE: FC went to tea with Gertrude Stein and her companion Alice B. Toklas in Paris in 1922. The legend that Stein threw her out of the apartment because FC asked for the recipe of Miss Toklas's chocolate cake cannot be trusted. FC did not like chocolate in any form.

FLORA: 'Then I met my painter . . .'

DAS: Miss Crewe, may I congratulate you on your lecture. I found it most interesting!

FLORA: Thank you . . .!

DAS: I was surprised you did not mention Virginia Woolf.

FLORA: I seldom do.

DAS: Have you met George Bernard Shaw?

FLORA: Yes. I was nearly in one of his plays once.

DAS: But you are not an actress . . .?

FLORA: No, that was the trouble.

DAS: What do you think of Jummapur?

FLORA: Well, I only arrived the day before yesterday but –

DAS: Of course. How absurd of me!

FLORA: Not at all. I was going to say that my first impression –

DAS: Jummapur is not in any case to be compared with London. Do you live in Bloomsbury?

FLORA: No, I live in Chelsea.

DAS: Chelsea – of course! My favourite part of London!

FLORA: Oh! You . . .?

DAS: I hope to visit London one of these days. The Chelsea of Turner and the Pre-Raphaelite Brotherhood! – Rossetti lived in Cheen Walk! Holman Hunt lived in Old Church Street! 'The Hireling Shepherd' was *painted* in Old Church Street! What an inspiration it would be to me to visit Chelsea!

FLORA: You are a painter!

DAS: Yes! Nirad Das.

FLORA: How do you do?

DAS: I am top hole. Thank you. May I give you a present?

FLORA: Oh . . .

DAS: Please do not judge it too harshly, Miss Crewe . . .

FLORA: Thank you!

DAS: Of course, I work in oils, Winsor and Newton. If it would please you to sit for your portrait I would like to repay you for your superfine portrait-in-words of the rough-and-tumble of literary life in London.

FLORA: Would you really?

DAS: I would very much!

(DAS *produces a small sketch pad and tears off a sheet. He gives it to her shyly.*)

FLORA: '. . . and he gave me a pencil sketch of myself holding forth on the literary life.'

(FLORA *retraces her steps with* COOMARASWAMI.)

PIKE: She mentions a pencil sketch. Do you know what happened to it?

MRS SWAN: I'm sure I never saw it. I would have remembered if it had been among what was called her effects. It was only one suitcase.

PIKE: Do you still have it?

MRS SWAN: What? Her suitcase? Heavens, it was a battered old thing even then, and being always on the move, Eric and I, one shed things . . .

PIKE: You threw away Flora Crewe's suitcase?

MRS SWAN: What is it you're up to, Eldon? A *luggage* museum? Really, you're like an old woman about her; except, of course, that I'm not.

PIKE: But she was Flora Crewe!

MRS SWAN: (*Crisply*) Well, if so, where was everybody sixty years ago?

(MRS SWAN *replenishes the teacups.* PIKE *takes one or two more letters from the shoebox and scans them.*

At the guesthouse, NIRAD DAS *arrives by bicycle. He has his wooden workbox strapped to the pillion-rack. His folded easel is strapped to his back. He rides one-handed, holding a canvas in his free hand.*

FLORA, *in her cornflower-blue dress, comes out from the interior.*)

FLORA: Good morning!

DAS: Miss Crewe! Here I am! A little late! Forgive me!

FLORA: I didn't realize – I've been writing a letter. Does this look all right?

DAS: (*Nervously*) Very, very good.

FLORA: Now . . . this *will* be nice, we'll both be working. Poet and painter. Work in progress.

(DAS *unstraps his work-box and establishes himself on the verandah.* FLORA *establishes herself at her work table.* PIKE *is puzzling over a letter.*)

PIKE: She says paint on paper.

MRS SWAN: Yes.

PIKE: '. . . a smudge of paint on paper . . .' – 'Perhaps my soul will stay behind as a smudge of paint on paper' . . . She's referring to an actual painting, isn't she?

MRS SWAN: I don't know.

PIKE: And 'undressed'. She says 'undressed'. Like a nude. On *paper*. That would be a watercolour, wouldn't it?

MRS SWAN: What would? There isn't any 'it'.

PIKE: Well, if it doesn't mean a portrait of Flora undressed, what do you think it means?

MRS SWAN: As much or as little as you like. Isn't that the point of being a poet?

PIKE: I don't know, I'm not a poet, but it reads quite specific, the deserted house . . . where is the bit?

MRS SWAN: Between your teeth, Eldon.

PIKE: Here. 'In an empty house . . .' – 'Perhaps my soul will stay behind as a smudge of paint on paper, as if I'd always been here, like . . . Radha?'

MRS SWAN: Radha.

PIKE: '– the most beautiful of the herdswomen, undressed –'

MRS SWAN: (*Interrupting, briskly*) Well, the portrait, as it happens, is on canvas and Flora is wearing her cornflower dress.

PIKE: Portrait?

MRS SWAN: She mentions the portrait somewhere. It was rolled up in the suitcase.

PIKE: Eleanor . . . do you mean there's a portrait of Flora?

MRS SWAN: Would you like to see it?

PIKE: Oh my God.

9

MRS SWAN: It's fairly ghastly, like an Indian cinema poster. I
think I know where it is but I'll need you to get it down for
me. Should we go in? We're about to lose the sun.

PIKE: Oh my God. But this is . . . Oh my God. There's never
been one, not a real portrait.

MRS SWAN: That's true. Apart from the Paris portrait; but that
was on canvas, too.

PIKE: The *Paris* portrait . . .?

MRS SWAN: Yes, Flora's first time in Paris, she was driving an
ambulance, officially, in the last year of the '14–'18 war . . .
so she was twenty-three, I suppose, when she met
Modigliani.

PIKE: Modigliani?!

MRS SWAN: Oh, Flora met everybody. Not that Modigliani was
anybody at the time.

PIKE: *A portrait by Modigliani?*

MRS SWAN: I was nine at the Armistice, so that was, my
goodness, sixty-six years ago! I'm coming up to seventy-five,
you know.

PIKE: Eleanor . . . I can hardly believe my ears.

MRS SWAN: I'm afraid so. I was born in 1909. But thank you,
Eldon. Have another slice of cake.

PIKE: No – thank you – I – excuse me: a painting of Flora by
Modigli –

MRS SWAN: Yes. A nude.

PIKE: (*Reverently*) A nude!

MRS SWAN: I never saw it myself. I was at school, of course, and
then, it was too late.

PIKE: Too late?

MRS SWAN: Yes, isn't that bad luck? The Technicolor Flora like
a cork in a storm, washed up on top of a wardrobe in a
bungalow in Shepperton, and the Modigliani, which would
have paid for the bungalow several times over, burned to
ashes in a bathtub in the Ritz.

(*By now she has assembled the tea-tray and she leaves with it.*)

PIKE: Could you run that by me again?

(PIKE *totters after her.*

FLORA, *in her blue dress, is at the table on the verandah, writing in her notebook with a fountain pen. She pauses, thinking, sitting quite still. Her feet are bare and her shoes are placed neatly to one side.* DAS *is painting her portrait.*)

FLORA: (*Recorded*) 'Yes I am in heat like a bride in a bath,
      without secrets, soaked in heated air
      that liquifies to the touch and floods,
      shortening the breath, yes
      I am discovered, heat has found me out,
      a stain that stops at nothing,
      not the squeezed gates or soft gutters,
      it slicks into the press
      that prints me to the sheet
      yes, think of a woman in a house of net
      that strains the oxygen out of the air
      thickening the night to Indian ink
      or think if you prefer – '
      (FLORA *has unconsciously crossed her legs, which brings* DAS's *work to a halt. He waits, patiently.*
      She notices that DAS *has stopped.*)
      Oh . . .

DAS: No, please be comfortable.

FLORA: I'm sorry! (*She puts her feet side-by-side.*) There. Is that how I was?

DAS: You are patient with me. I think your nature is very kind.

FLORA: Do you think so, Mr Das?

DAS: I am sure of it. May I ask you a personal question?

FLORA: That *is* a personal question.

DAS: Oh my goodness, is it?

FLORA: I always think so. It always feels like one. Carte blanche is what you're asking, Mr Das. Am I to lay myself bare before you?

DAS: (*Panicking slightly*) My question was only about your poem!

FLORA: At least you knew it was personal.

DAS: I will not ask it now, of course.

FLORA: On that understanding I will answer it. My poem is about heat.

DAS: Oh. Thank you.

FLORA: I resume my pose. Pen to paper. Legs uncrossed. You

know, you are the first man to paint my toe-nails.

DAS: Actually, I am occupied in the folds of your skirt.

FLORA: Ah. In that you are not the first.

DAS: You have been painted before? – but of course you have! Many times, I expect!

FLORA: You know, Mr Das, your nature is much kinder than mine.

(FLORA *resumes*. DAS *resumes*.

ANISH DAS *comes into the Shepperton garden. He has a soft briefcase; he sits in one of the garden chairs*.)

Mr Das, I have been considering whether to ask you a delicate question, as between friends and artists.

DAS: Oh, Miss Crewe, I am transported beyond my most fantastical hopes of our fellowship! This is a red-letter day without dispute!

FLORA: If you are going to be so Indian I shan't ask it.

DAS: But I cannot be less Indian that I am.

FLORA: You could if you tried. I'm not sure I'm going to ask you now.

DAS: Then you need not, dear Miss Crewe! You considered. The unasked, the almost asked question, united us for a moment in its intimacy, we came together in your mind like a spark in a vacuum glass, and the redness of the day's letter will not be denied.

FLORA: You are still doing it, Mr Das.

DAS: You wish me to be less Indian?

FLORA: I did say that but I think what I meant was for you to be *more* Indian, or at any rate *Indian*, not Englished-up and all over me like a labrador and knocking things off tables with your tail – so *waggish* of you, Mr Das, to compare my mind to a vacuum. You only do it with us, I don't believe that left to yourself you can't have an ordinary conversation without jumping backwards through hoops of delight, *with* whoops of delight, I think I mean; actually, I do know what I mean, I want you to be with me as you would be if *I* were Indian.

DAS: An Indian Miss Crewe! Oh dear, that is a mental construction which has no counterpart in the material world.

FLORA: So is a *unicorn*, but you can imagine it.

DAS: You can imagine it but you cannot mount it.

FLORA: Imagining it was all I was asking in my case.

DAS: (*Terribly discomfited*) Oh! Oh, my gracious! – I had no
intention – I assure you –

FLORA: (*Amused*) No, no, you cannot unwag your very best wag.
You cleared the table, the bric-a-brac is on the Wilton – the
specimen vase, the snuff box, the souvenir of Broadstairs –
(*But she has misjudged.*)

DAS: (*Anguished*) You are cruel to me, Miss Crewe!

FLORA: (*Instantly repentant*) Oh! I'm so sorry. I didn't want to be.
It's my nature. Please come out from behind your easel –
look at me.

DAS: May we fall silent, please. I prefer to work in silence.

FLORA: I've spoiled everything. I'm very sorry.

DAS: The shadow has moved. I must correct it.

FLORA: Yes, it has moved. It cannot be corrected. We must wait
for tomorrow. I'm so sorry.

(DAS *resumes working at the easel.* FLORA *maintains her pose,
but screws the cap on to her fountain pen.*

ANISH *stands up at the approach of* MRS SWAN *who comes from
the bungalow with tea for two on a tray, and two kinds of cake.*)

ANISH: Let me help you.

MRS SWAN: I've forgotten your sugar.

ANISH: Actually, I don't take it.

MRS SWAN: Oh. I thought you'd be more Indian.

(*They settle the tray and themselves at the garden table.*)

ANISH: This is so kind of you.

MRS SWAN: Oh no. Your letter was irresistible. Having an artist
to tea was beyond my fondest hopes for my dotage. We'll let
it sit a minute. Do you think you take after your father?

ANISH: I don't know. I would like to think so. But my father was
a man who suffered for his beliefs and I have never had to do
that, so perhaps I will never know.

MRS SWAN: I really meant being a painter. You are a painter like
your father.

ANISH: Oh . . . yes. Yes, I am a painter like my father. Though
not at all like my father, of course.

13

MRS SWAN: Your father was an Indian painter, you mean?

ANISH: An Indian painter? Well, I'm as Indian as he was. But yes. I suppose I am not a particularly *Indian* painter . . . not an Indian painter *particularly*, or rather . . .

MRS SWAN: Not particularly an Indian painter.

ANISH: Yes. But then, nor was he. Apart from being Indian.

MRS SWAN: As you are.

ANISH: Yes.

MRS SWAN: Though you are not at all like him.

ANISH: No. Yes. My father was a quite different kind of artist, a portrait painter, as you know . . .

MRS SWAN: I can't say I do, Mr Das. Until I received your letter your father was unknown to me. In fact, the attribution 'Unknown Indian Artist' described the situation exactly . . .

ANISH: He was not unknown in Jummapur!

MRS SWAN: . . . if indeed it was your father who did the portrait of Flora.

ANISH: Oh, the portrait is certainly my father's work, Mrs Swan! You cannot imagine my feelings when I saw the book in the shop window – my excitement! You see, I carry my copy everywhere.

(*He takes* The Collected Letters *from his briefcase. The dustjacket has the portrait of Flora by Nirad Das.*)

MRS SWAN: Well, I hope there'll be lots like *you*, Mr Das.

ANISH: There will be no one like me, Mrs Swan! It was not the book, of course, but the painting on the jacket and reproduced inside. If only he could have known that one day his portrait of Flora Crewe . . .

MRS SWAN: He might have been more pleased to be in the window of an art gallery than a bookshop.

ANISH: Perhaps not. I'm sure my father never had a single one of his paintings reproduced, and that is an extraordinary pleasure for an artist. I know! The painting under one's hand is everything, of course . . . unique. But replication! *That* is popularity! Put us on book jackets – calendars – biscuit tins! Oh, he would have been quite proud!

MRS SWAN: By the way, what *were* your father's beliefs?

ANISH: (*Surprised*) Why . . . we are Hindu . . .

14

MRS SWAN: You said he had suffered for his beliefs.

ANISH: Oh. I meant his opinions.

MRS SWAN: How did he suffer?

ANISH: He was put in prison.

MRS SWAN: Really? By whom?

ANISH: Well, by you.

MRS SWAN: By me? Oh . . . by us. But how did we know what his opinions were?

ANISH: It seems he took part in some actions against the Raj during the Empire Day celebrations in Jummapur.

MRS SWAN: Then he was put in prison for his actions, not his opinions, Mr Das, and obviously deserved what he got. Will you have a slice of cake?

ANISH: Thank you.

MRS SWAN: Victoria sponge or Battenberg?

ANISH: Oh . . .

MRS SWAN: The sponge is my own, raspberry jam included.

ANISH: I would love some . . . thank you.

MRS SWAN: Tea? But all that must have been before you were born.

ANISH: Oh, yes, I was the child of my father's second marriage. I was born long after Independence, and my father went to prison in Jummapur in 1930.

MRS SWAN: 1930! But that was when Flora was in Jummapur!

ANISH: Yes, I know. That is why I am here.

(MRS SWAN *administers tea.*

FLORA *takes the cap off her fountain pen.*)

FLORA: Are we friends this morning?

DAS: I hope so! Why do you ask that? Has something happened?

FLORA: Oh. No.

(*She laughs. He frowns, painting.*)

Well, I thought if we're friends I'll ask you to write something on the drawing you did of me.

(*She produces the pencil sketch.*)

DAS: Oh, but that was only a poor scribble! Not even a good likeness!

FLORA: Even so.

DAS: Oh.

(*He is taken aback but then realizes he is being teased. He laughs.*)

FLORA: Yes, you won't get anywhere with that.

(NAZRUL, *the servant, brings a jug of fresh lemonade and two glasses, which he puts on the table.*)

Namby pani time!

NAZRUL: Nimbupani!

FLORA: (*Getting up*) Thank you, Nazrul . . . Shukriya!

(NAZRUL *responds and leaves.*)

DAS: Actually, I have something for you, a little present.

FLORA: Have you? You mustn't keep giving me things, Mr Das!

DAS: Well, it is a kind of birthday present, you see.

FLORA: Especially not birthday presents when it isn't my birthday.

(DAS *gives her an old but well-preserved book. It is green with a brown spine. In fact it is a copy of* Up the Country *by Emily Eden [1866].*)

DAS: I did not buy it, it is a book of my father's which I would like you to have. Letters by an English lady travelling in India a hundred years ago.

FLORA: (*Truly pleased*) Oh, but this will be just my book! Thank you! *Up the Country* . . . Emily Eden. Oh, it's a lovely present!

DAS: Well . . . I will write, 'To remind you of Jummapur and your friend and fellow artist Nirad Das'. And I will draw myself listening to you.

(FLORA *pours the nimbupani.* DAS *writes on the pencil drawing with his own fountain pen, and settles down to draw her.*)

ANISH: When my father met Flora Crewe he had been a widower for several years, although he was still quite a young man, younger than her, yes, the beginning of the Hot Weather in 1930 . . . he had his 34th birthday on April 2nd, just after he met your sister. He had lost his wife to cholera and he was childless. I knew nothing of my father's life before me. In my earliest memory, my father was an old gentleman who spoke very little except when he sometimes read aloud to me. He liked to read in English. Robert Browning, Tennyson, Macaulay's *Lays of Ancient Rome*, and Dickens, of course . . .

MRS SWAN: How surprising.

ANISH: Oh yes – he went from a vernacular school to Elphinstone

College in Bombay, and you only have to look at Elphinstone College to see that it was built to give us a proper English education.

MRS SWAN: I meant, in view of his 'opinions'. But I spoke without thinking. Your father took part in actions against the British Raj and loved English literature, which was perfectly consistent of him.

ANISH: (*Laughs*) Usually, the education succeeded admirably! In Jummapur we were 'loyal' as you would say, we had been loyal to the British right through the first War of Independence.

MRS SWAN: The . . .? What war was that?

ANISH: The Rising of 1857.

MRS SWAN: Oh, you mean the Mutiny. *What* did you call it?

ANISH: Dear Mrs Swan, Imperial history is merely . . . no, no – I promise you I didn't come to give you a history lesson.

MRS SWAN: You seem ill-equipped to do so. We were your Romans, you know. We might have been your Normans.

ANISH: And did you expect us to be grateful?

MRS SWAN: That's neither here nor there. I don't suppose I'd have been grateful if a lot of Romans turned up and started laying down the law and teaching Latin and so forth. 'What a cheek,' is probably what I would have thought. 'Go away, and take your roads and your baths with you.' It doesn't matter what I would have thought. It's what I think now that matters. You speak English better than most young people I meet. Did you go to school here?

ANISH: No, I went to a convent school in . . . You are spreading a net for me, Mrs Swan!

MRS SWAN: What net would that be? Have some more cake.

ANISH: Mrs Swan, you are a very wicked woman. You advance a preposterous argument and try to fill my mouth with cake so I cannot answer you. I will resist you and your cake. *We* were the Romans! We were up to date when you were a backward nation. The foreigners who invaded *you* found a third-world country! Even when you discovered India in the age of Shakespeare, we already had our Shakespeares. And our science – architecture – our literature and art, we had a

17

culture older and more splendid, we were rich! After all, that's why you came.

(*But he has misjudged.*)

MRS SWAN: (*Angrily*) We made you a proper country! And when we left you fell straight to pieces like Humpty Dumpty! Look at the map! You should feel nothing but shame!

ANISH: Oh, yes . . . I am a guest here and I have been . . .

MRS SWAN: (*Calming down*) No, only provocative. Will you be going home?

ANISH: (*Bewildered*) I . . . would you like me to go?

MRS SWAN: (*Equally bewildered*) No. What do you mean?

ANISH: (*Understanding*) Oh – *home*! I didn't mean I was a guest in *England*. England is my home now. I have spent half my life here. I married here.

MRS SWAN: An English girl?

ANISH: Yes. We met at art school.

MRS SWAN: (*Approvingly*) Artists together.

ANISH: Actually she was not a student, she was earning money as a model. Life class, you see.

MRS SWAN: Of course. Is she still your model?

ANISH: No. My work is not figurative now.

MRS SWAN: What is it now?

ANISH: Well, deconstructive.

MRS SWAN: What a shame.

ANISH: I can still draw if I wish. May I draw you?

MRS SWAN: Oh no, the last thing I need –

ANISH: No, for myself.

MRS SWAN: Oh. Why?

ANISH: Only a little sketch with a pencil. We must not resist when life strives to close one of its many circles!

MRS SWAN: Is that Hinduism?

ANISH: DAS: Oh . . . I don't know. Perhaps.

MRS SWAN: Well, it sounds very east of Suez. All right then. You may draw me.

ANISH: It will make us friends.

(ANISH *takes an artist's block from his briefcase and begins to draw her.*

FLORA *and* DAS *sit at the table with lemonade.*)

FLORA: While having tiffin on the verandah of my bungalow I spilled kedgeree on my dungarees and had to go to the gymkhana in my pyjamas looking like a coolie.

DAS: I was buying chutney in the bazaar when a thug escaped from the choky and killed a box-wallah for his loot, creating a hullabaloo and landing himself in the mulligatawny.

FLORA: I went doolally at the durbar and was sent back to Blighty in a dooley feeling rather dikki with a cup of char and a chit for a chotapeg.

DAS: Yes, and the burra sahib who looked so pukka in his topee sent a coolie to the memshib –

FLORA: No, no. You can't have memsahib *and* sahib, that's cheating – and anyway I've already said coolie.

DAS: I concede, Miss Crewe. You are the Hobson-Jobson champion!

FLORA: You are chivalrous, Mr Das. So I'll confess I had help. I found a whole list of Anglo-Indian words in my bedside drawer, for the benefit of travellers.

DAS: But I know both languages, so you still win on handicap.

FLORA: Where did you learn everything, Mr Das?

DAS: From books. I like Dickens and Browning, and Shakespeare, of course – but my favourite is Agatha Christie! *The Mysterious Affair at Styles*! – oh, the woman is a genius! But I would like to write like Macaulay.

FLORA: Oh dear.

DAS: I have to thank Lord Macaulay for English, you know. It was his idea when he was in the government of India that English should be taught to us all. He wanted to supply the East India Company with clerks, but he was sowing dragon's teeth. Instead of babus he produced lawyers, journalists, civil servants, he produced Gandhi! We have so many, many languages, you know, that English is the only language the nationalists can communicate in! That is a very good joke on Macaulay, don't you think?

FLORA: Are *you* a nationalist, Mr Das?

DAS: (*Lightly*) Ah, that is a very interesting question! But we shouldn't have stopped all this time. It's getting late for you, I must work more quickly tomorrow.

FLORA: It's only half-past ten.

DAS: No, it's already April, and that is becoming late.

FLORA: Yes, it seems hotter than ever. Would you like some more lemonade?

DAS: No, thank you, no lemonade. Miss Crewe, you haven't looked at my painting yet.

FLORA: No. Not yet. I never look. Do you mind?

DAS: No.

FLORA: You do really. But I once asked a painter 'Can I look?' and he said, 'Why? When I paint a table I don't have to show it to the table.'

DAS: I said you had been painted before.

FLORA: Only once.

DAS: A portrait?

FLORA: Not in the way you mean. It was a nude.

DAS: Oh.

FLORA: Unusually. He painted his friends clothed. For nudes he used models. I believe I was his friend. But perhaps not. Perhaps a used model only. It hardly matters. He was dead so soon afterwards. (*Pause*) He was not so kind to me as you are.

DAS: Do you have the painting?

FLORA: No.

DAS: Where is it?

FLORA: Nowhere. A man I thought I might marry burned it. My goodness, what a red-letter day you are having. There's a man on a horse.

(*We have already heard the horse. We do not see the horse.*)

DURANCE: (*Offstage*) Good morning! Miss Crewe, I think!

FLORA: (*Standing up*) Yes – good morning! (*To* DAS) Do you know him?

DAS: He is the Assistant.

DURANCE: (*Offstage*) May I get down a moment?

FLORA: Of course. What a beautiful animal! (*To* DAS) Assistant what?

DAS: (*To* FLORA) Captain Durance!

DURANCE: Thank you!

FLORA: Come on up, do join us.

(DURANCE *arrives on foot.*)

DURANCE: Oh – it's Mr Das, isn't it?

DAS: Good morning, sir. But we have never met.

DURANCE: Oh, but I know you. And Miss Crewe, your fame
precedes you.

FLORA: Thank you . . . and you . . .

DURANCE: I'm from the Residency. David Durance.

FLORA: (*Shaking hands*) How do you do?

DURANCE: Oh, but look here – I'm interrupting the artist.

FLORA: We had stopped.

DURANCE: May one look? Oh, I say! Coming along jolly well!
Don't you think so, Miss Crewe?

DAS: I must be going. I have overstayed my time today.

FLORA: But we'll continue tomorrow?

DAS: Yes. Perhaps a little earlier if it suits you. I can leave
everything . . .

(DAS *prepares to remove the canvas from the easel.*)

FLORA: Why don't you leave the canvas too? It will be quite
safe.

DAS: (*Hesitates*) Yes, all right . . . I have a drape for it. Thank
you.

(*He drapes a cloth over the canvas on the easel.*)

FLORA: Like shutting up the parrot for the night.

DAS: There we are. Thank you for the lemonade, Miss Crewe.
An absolute treat. I promise you! Goodbye, sir – and – yes
– and until tomorrow . . .

(*He goes down the verandah steps and wheels his bicycle away.*)

FLORA: Yes . . . goodbye! (*To* DURANCE) I'll put my shoes on.
Sorry about my toes, but I like to wriggle them when I'm
working.

DURANCE: I'll only stay a moment. My chief asked me to look
in. Just to make sure there's nothing we can do for you.

FLORA: Would you like some lemonade?

DURANCE: No, nothing for me. Really. We might have found
you more comfortable quarters, you know, not quite so
in-the-town.

FLORA: How did you know I was here?

DURANCE: Now, there's a point. Usually we know of arrivals

because the first thing they do is drop in a card but in your case . . . rumours in the bazaar, so to speak. Are you an old hand here, Miss Crewe?

FLORA: No, I've never been to India before. I came up from Bombay just a few days ago.

DURANCE: But you have friends here, perhaps?

FLORA: No. I got on a ship and I came, knowing no-one. I have friends in England who have friends here. Actually, one friend.

DURANCE: In Jummapur, this friend?

FLORA: No – the *friend* – my friend – is in London, of course; Mr Joshua Chamberlain. *His* friends are in different places in Rajputana, and I will also be going to Delhi and then up to the Punjab, I hope.

DURANCE: Now I see. And your friend in London has friends in Jummapur.

FLORA: Yes.

DURANCE: Like Mr Das?

FLORA: No. Are you a policeman of some kind. Mr Durance?

DURANCE: Me? No. I'm sorry if I sound like one.

FLORA: Well, you do a bit. I'm travelling with letters of introduction to a number of social clubs and literary societies. I speak on the subject of 'Literary Life in London', in return for board and lodging . . . So you see I couldn't have taken advantage of your kindness without giving offence to my hosts.

DURANCE: The game is different here. By putting up at the Residency you would have gained respect, not lost it.

FLORA: Thank you, but what about self-respect?

DURANCE: Well . . . as long as all is well. So you are following in Chamberlain's footsteps. All is explained.

FLORA: I don't think *I* explained it. But yes, I am. He spoke in Jummapur three years ago, on the subject of Empire.

DURANCE: Yes. Is he a good friend?

FLORA: Well . . .

DURANCE: Did you know he was some sort of Communist?

FLORA: I thought he might be. He stood twice for Parliament as the Communist candidate.

22

DURANCE: (*Unoffended, pleasant as before*) I amuse you. That's all right, amusing our distinguished visitors is among my duties.

FLORA: Well, don't be so stuffy.

DURANCE: How long will you be with us?

FLORA: I'm expected in Jaipur but they don't mind when I come.

DURANCE: I'm sure you'll have a marvellous time. There are wonderful things to see. Meanwhile, please consider yourself an honorary member of the Club – mention my name, but I'll put you in the book.

FLORA: Thank you.

DURANCE: Well . . .

(*He offers his hand and she shakes it.*)

FLORA: Call again, if you like. I wish I had a lump of sugar for your horse. Next time.

DURANCE: He's my main indulgence. I wish I'd been here when a good horse went with the job.

FLORA: Yes . . . what *is* your job? You mentioned your chief.

DURANCE: The Resident. He represents the government here.

FLORA: The British government?

DURANCE: Delhi. The Viceroy, in fact. Jummapur is not British India . . . you understand that?

FLORA: Yes . . . but it's all the Empire, isn't it?

DURANCE: Oh yes. Absolutely. But there's about five hundred Rajahs and Maharajahs and Nabobs and so on who run bits of it, well, nearly half of it, actually, by treaty. And we're here to make sure they don't get up to mischief.

FLORA: I knew you were a kind of policeman.

(DURANCE *laughs and goes down the steps of the verandah. He hesitates shyly.*)

DURANCE: Miss Crewe, would you have dinner with us while you are here?

FLORA: With you and your wife, do you mean?

DURANCE: No . . . at the Club. Us. With me. I don't run to a wife, I'm afraid. But do come. We're a reasonably civilized lot, and there's usually dancing on Saturdays, only a gramophone but lots of fun.

FLORA: I'd love to. On Saturday, then.

23

DURANCE: Oh . . . splendid! I'll come by.

FLORA: I haven't got a horse, you know.

DURANCE: We have a Daimler at the Residency. I'll see if I can wangle it. Pick you up about eight?

FLORA: Yes.

DURANCE: We don't dress, normally, except on dress nights.
(*Laughs at himself*) Obviously.

FLORA: I'll be ready.

DURANCE: Jolly good.
(*He exits and mounts the horse which snorts.*)

FLORA: Goodbye!

DURANCE: (*Offstage*) Goodbye!

FLORA: (*Calling out*) Wangle the Daimler!
(FLORA *waves and turns aside. She sits at her table and starts to write.*
ANISH *is drawing* MRS SWAN.)

MRS SWAN: But Jummapur was a Native State.

ANISH: Yes.

MRS SWAN: So *we* didn't put your father in gaol.

ANISH: (*Politely dissenting*) Ah well . . .

MRS SWAN: (*Firmly*) Whatever your father may have done, the Resident would have had no authority to imprison an Indian. The Rajah of Jummapur had his own justice.

ANISH: Ah, but His Highness the Rajah . . .

MRS SWAN: Oh, I'm not saying we wouldn't have boxed his ears and sent him packing if he forgot which side his bread was buttered, but facts are facts. The Rajah put your father in the choky. How long for, by the way?

ANISH: Six months.

MRS SWAN: There you are. In British India he would have got a year at least. After the War it may have been different. With Independence round the corner, people were queuing up to go to prison, it was their ticket to the top. They'd do their bit of civil disobedience and hop into the paddy-waggon thoroughly pleased with themselves. Eric – that's my husband – would let them off with a small fine if he thought they were Johnny-come-latelies, and they'd be furious. That was when Eric had his District. We were right up near Nepal . . .

24

ANISH: Yes, the tea-tray . . .

MRS SWAN: You spotted it. In India we had pictures of coaching inns and foxhunting, and now I've landed up in Shepperton I've got elephants and prayer wheels cluttering up the window ledges, and the tea-tray is Nepalese brass. One could make a comment about human nature but have a slice of Battenburg instead.

ANISH: Thank you.

MRS SWAN: I got it specially, an artistic sort of cake, I always think. What kind of paintings are they, these paintings that are not like your father's? Describe your latest. Like the cake?

ANISH: (*Eating*) Delicious. Thank you.

MRS SWAN: No, are they like the cake?

ANISH: Oh. No. They are all . . . like each other really. I can't *describe* them.

MRS SWAN: Indescribable, then.

(ANISH *completes the drawing, and passes it to her*.)

ANISH: There.

MRS SWAN: (*Pleasantly surprised*) Ah. That's a proper drawing. You could do portraits if you wanted.

(*She gives the drawing back to* ANISH.)

ANISH: Thank you.

MRS SWAN: Now, what are we going to tell Eldon about your father?

ANISH: Eldon?

MRS SWAN: E. Cooper Pike. He calls me Eleanor so I have to call him Eldon, so as not to seem toffee-nosed. If he starts calling me Nell I suppose I'll have to call him El. He's waiting for me to die so he can get on with Flora's biography which he thinks I don't know he's writing.

ANISH: (*Referring to his copy of the book*) Oh yes. 'Edited by E. Cooper Pike.'

MRS SWAN: That means he does the footnotes.

ANISH: Oh yes, I see.

MRS SWAN: Far too much of a good thing, in my opinion, the footnotes; to be constantly interrupted by someone telling you things you already know or don't need to know at that moment. There are pages where Flora can hardly get a word in sideways. Mr Pike teaches Flora Crewe. It makes her sound like a subject, doesn't it, like biology. Or in her case, botany. Flora is widely taught in America. I have been written to, even visited, and on one occasion telephoned, by young women doing Flora Crewe. Almost always young women. And from all over, lots from America. Flora has become quite a heroine. Which she always was to me. I was only three when Mother died, so it was Flora who . . . Oh dear, I'm going to need a hanky.

ANISH: Oh – I say! I'm sorry –

MRS SWAN: Found it. (*She blows her nose.*) It makes me so cross that she missed it all, the *Collected Poems*, and now the *Letters*, with her name all over the place and students and professors so *interested* and so sweet about her poetry. Nobody gave tuppence about her while she was alive except to get her knickers off. How is your tea?

(DAS *arrives at the guesthouse and props his bicycle against the verandah.* FLORA, *working, barely acknowledges him.*)

ANISH: It's very nice. Mrs Swan . . . it says, 'The portrait of Flora Crewe is reproduced by permission of Mrs Eleanor Swan.' Does that mean you have it?

MRS SWAN: Yes.

ANISH: Here? In your house?

MRS SWAN: Would you like to see it?

ANISH: Very much! I half expected to see it hanging the moment I arrived.

MRS SWAN: That's because you're a painter. I'll bring it out. Yes, I can't get the tea here to taste as it should. I expect it's the water. A reservoir near Staines won't have the makings of a good cup of tea compared to the water we got in the Hills. It came straight off the Himalayas.

(*She leaves.*

FLORA *and* DAS *are at work.*)

FLORA: (*Recorded*)

'. . . yes, think of a woman in a blue dress
sat on a straight-backed chair at a plain table
on the verandah of a guesthouse,

writing about the weather.
Or think, if you prefer, of bitches,
cats, goats, monkeys at it like –'
Oh, fiddlesticks! May we stop for a moment. (FLORA *gets up*.) I'm sticking to myself.

DAS: Of course! Forgive me!

FLORA: You mustn't take responsibility for the climate too, Mr Das.

DAS: No, I . . .

FLORA: No, I'm sorry. I'm bad tempered. Should we have some tea? I wouldn't mind something to eat too. (*Calls out*) Nazrul! (*To* DAS) There's a jar of duck pâté in the refrigerator . . .
(NAZRUL *appears from round the corner of the verandah*.)
Oh, Nazrul . . . char and . . .

NAZRUL: (*In Hindi*) Yes, madam, I will bring tea immediately . . .

FLORA: . . . bread . . . and in the icebox, no, don't go, listen to me –

DAS: Would you allow me, please?
(DAS *and* NAZRUL *speak in Hindi.* DAS *orders bread and butter and the duck pâté from the fridge.*)

FLORA: (*Over the conversation*) A jar with a picture of a *duck* . . .
(*But* NAZRUL *has dramatic and tragic disclosures to make. Thieves have stolen the pâté.* DAS *berates him.* NAZRUL *leaves the way he came.*)
What was all that?

DAS: He will bring tea, and bread and butter and cake. The pâté has been taken by robbers.

FLORA: What?!

DAS: (*Gravely*) Just so, I'm afraid.

FLORA: But the refrigerator is padlocked – Mr Coomraswami pointed it out to me particularly.

DAS: Where do you keep the key?

FLORA: Nazrul keeps it, of course.

DAS: Ah well . . . the whole thing is a great mystery.
(FLORA *splutters into laughter and* DAS *joins in.*)

FLORA: But surely, isn't it against his religion?

DAS: Oh, certainly. I should say so. Not that I'm saying Nazrul stole the pâté, but stealing would be against his religion, undoubtedly.

FLORA: I don't mean stealing, I mean the pork.

DAS: But I thought you said it was duck.

FLORA: One must read the small print, Mr Das. 'Duck pâté' in large letters, 'with pork' in small letters. It's normal commercial practice.

DAS: Yes, I see.

FLORA: We must hope he only got the duck part . . .

DAS: That is your true nature speaking, Miss Crewe!

FLORA: . . . though of course, if they use one pig for every duck, he'll be lucky to have got any duck at all.

DAS: The truth will never be known, only to God who is merciful.

FLORA: Yes. Which God do you mean?

DAS: Yours if you wish, by all means.

FLORA: Now, Mr Das, there is such a thing as being too polite. Yours was here first.

DAS: Oh, but we Hindus can afford to be generous; we have gods to spare, one for every occasion. And Krishna said, 'Whichever god a man worships, it is I who answers the prayer.'

FLORA: I wasn't sure whether Krishna was a god or a person.

DAS: Oh, he was most certainly a god, one of the ten incarnations of Vishnu. He had a great love affair, you see, with a married lady, Radha.

FLORA: I think that's what confused me.

DAS: Radha was the most beautiful of the herdswomen. She fell passionately in love with Krishna. She would often escape from her husband to meet him in secret. It is a favourite subject of the old Rajasthani painters.

FLORA: Come and sit down, Mr Das.

DAS: I will . . . but I will start on my tree while we wait.

FLORA: Put a monkey in it.

DAS: Yes. Like Hanuman, he is my favourite in the Ramayana. The monkey god.

FLORA: Mr Coomaraswami showed me the temples.

DAS: Did you find them interesting?

FLORA: I liked some of the sculptures, the way the women are often smiling to themselves. Yes, that was quite revealing, I thought.

DAS: About Indian women?

FLORA: No, about Indian sculptors. And breasts like melons, and baby-bearing hips. You must think me ill-favoured.

DAS: No. My wife was slightly built.

FLORA: Oh . . .

(NAZRUL *enters with the tea-tray*.)

FLORA: Thank you, Nazrul . . . And two kinds of cake!

(NAZRUL *replies smilingly and leaves*.)

DAS: But your face today . . . I think your work was troublesome.

FLORA: Yes.

DAS: Is it the rhyming that is difficult?

FLORA: No.

DAS: The metre?

FLORA: No. The . . . emotion won't harmonize. I'm afraid I'm not much good at talking about it.

DAS: I'm sorry.

FLORA: That's why I don't keep nipping round to your side of the easel. If I don't look there's nothing to say. I think that that's better.

DAS: Yes. It is better to wait. My painting has no *rasa* today.

FLORA: What is *rasa*?

DAS: *Rasa* is juice. Its taste. Its essence. A painting must have its *rasa* . . . which is not *in* the painting exactly. *Rasa* is what you must feel when you see a painting, or hear music; it is the emotion which the artist must arouse in you.

FLORA: And poetry? Does a poem have *rasa*?

DAS: Oh yes! Poetry is a sentence whose soul is *rasa*. That is a famous dictum of Vishvanata, a great teacher of poetry, six hundred years ago.

FLORA: *Rasa* . . . yes. My poem has no *rasa*.

DAS: Or perhaps it has two *rasa* which are in conflict.

FLORA: Oh . . .

DAS: There are nine *rasa*, each one a different colour. I should say mood. But each mood has its colour – white for laughter and fun, red for anger, pale yellow for tranquillity . . .

FLORA: (*Interrupting*) Oh . . . is there one for grey?

DAS: Grey is for sorrow.

FLORA: Sorrow? I see.

DAS: Each one has its own name and its own god, too.

FLORA: And some don't get on, is that it?

DAS: Yes. That is it. Some do and some don't. If you arouse emotions which are in opposition to each other the *rasa* will not . . . harmonize, you said.

FLORA: Yes.

DAS: Your poem is about heat.

FLORA: Yes.

DAS: But its *rasa* is perhaps . . . anger?

FLORA: Sex.

DAS: (*Unhesitatingly*) The *rasa* of erotic love is called Shringara. Its god is Vishnu, and its colour is *shyama*, which is blue-black. Vishvanata in his book on poetics tells us: Shringara requires, naturally, a lover and his loved one, who may be a courtesan if she is sincerely enamoured, and it is aroused by, for example, the moon, the scent of sandalwood, or being in an empty house. Shringara goes harmoniously with all other *rasa* and their complementary emotions, with the exception of fear, cruelty, disgust and sloth.

FLORA: I see. Thank you. Empty house is very good. Mr Das, you sounded just like somebody else. Yourself, I expect. I knew you could. The other one reminded me of Dr Aziz in Forster's novel. Have you read it? I kept wanting to kick him.

DAS: (*Offended*) Oh . . .

FLORA: For not knowing his worth.

DAS: Then perhaps you didn't finish it.

FLORA: Yes, perhaps. Does he improve?

DAS: He alters.

FLORA: What is your opinion of *A Passage To India*?

DAS: Was that the delicate question you considered to ask me?

FLORA: (*Laughs happily*) Oh, Mr Das!

(PIKE *enters, dressed for India. He is staying at the best hotel in Jummapur, and looks it. He carries a smart shoulder-bag. He stares around him in a vaguely disappointed way.*

30

Modern street sounds, distinctly Indian, accompany PIKE's
entrance.

Flora is at her table, writing. DAS *is at the easel, painting.*)

FLORA: (*Writing*) 'Jummapur, Saturday April 5th. Darling Nell.
I'm having my portrait painted, I mean the painter is at it as I
write, so if you see a picture of me in my cornflower dress
you'll know I was writing *this* – some of the time anyway. He
thinks I'm writing a poem. Posing as a poet, you see, just as
the Enemy once said of me in his rotten rag.'

PIKE: 'The Enemy' was J. C. Squire (1884–1958), poet, critic,
literary editor of the *New Statesman* and editor of the *London
Mercury*. An anonymous editorial in the *London Mercury*
(April 1920) complained about, 'an outbreak of versifying
flappers who should stop posing as poets and confine
themselves to posing as railway stations'. The magazine was
sued by the poets Elizabeth Paddington (1901–1980) and
Meredith Euston (1899–1929), both cases being settled out
of court. FC poured a pint of beer over Squire's head in the
Fitzroy Tavern in January 1921.

(DILIP *enters with a bottle of cola.*)

DILIP: Dr Pike . . .

PIKE: Eldon, please.

DILIP: . . . will you have a cola, Eldon?

PIKE: Oh, thanks. What kind of . . .

(*His suspicion has been aroused.*)

Thumbs Up Cola? You know, I think maybe I won't.

DILIP: (*Misunderstanding*) I got two – really – I drank mine while I
was talking to the shopkeeper. It is as I thought. The dak
bungalow was exactly here, in the courtyard. Of course, the
flats did not exist. I'm afraid nothing you can see goes back
to before the war.

PIKE: No . . . That's a shame.

DILIP: Except the tree, perhaps.

PIKE: (*Brightening*) Oh, yes. The tree. That's right. She mentions
a tree.

DILIP: The old man remembers the bungalow very well. It was
destroyed. A casualty of Partition.

PIKE: Taken apart?

DILIP: Burned, in the riots. There were many people killed here in '47.

PIKE: *Partition*. Oh, yes . . . terrible . . . Would this be the same tree?

DILIP: Probably. It looks old.

PIKE: Would you take my picture? . . . on the spot.

DILIP: Yes, certainly.

PIKE: This is so good of you, Dilip.

DILIP: No, no, it is a red letter day for the fellowship of teachers of English literature!

(PIKE *takes a camera from his bag and gives it to* DILIP)

PIKE: It's self-focusing . . . just press the . . . (*He positions himself.*) I could take out an ad . . . in the newspaper. Someone may remember an artist . . . Go back a bit . . . show more of the . . .

DILIP: No, the 35 is fine. Do you mind if I take it off auto? . . . stop it down for the background . . . F8 . . .

PIKE: Oh . . . sure.

DILIP: Yes, why not? – put an advert in the paper. Ready? (*He takes the photo.*)

PIKE: Thank you. I'll take one of you.

DILIP: All right. (*Adjusting the camera*) On 50. More of Dilip. (*They change places,* PIKE *taking the camera. Dilip has a bag from which he takes* The Collected Letters of Flora Crewe, *to hold it for his photograph.*)

After all . . . fifty-six years . . . he could be still alive . . . he'd only have to be . . .

PIKE: Ninety.

DILIP: Yes, probably not. Is this all right?

PIKE: The other thing is . . . What do I do?

DILIP: Just point it.

PIKE: The other thing is, Dilip . . . Here we go. (*He takes the picture.*)

DILIP: Thank you.

PIKE: The other thing is, there was the watercolour. A lost portrait, a nude. That's the way it reads to *me*. Don't you think so?

DILIP: (*Laughs*) Oh yes, I think that's the way it reads to you,

32

Eldon, but she was a poet . . . and you're a biographer! A lost
portrait would be just the ticket.

PIKE: How about offering a reward?

DILIP: A reward?

PIKE: For information leading to. If the local paper did a story
about it . . . I bet that would get results.

DILIP: Undoubtedly. Your hotel will be stormed by a mob
waving authentic watercolour portraits of English ladies in
every stage of undress.

PIKE: I should get a shot from above, with the tree . . . Could one
get on the roof, do you think?

DILIP: I'm sure. Let me go and see.

(DILIP *leaves*.)

FLORA: 'Darling, you musn't expect me to be Intelligence from
Abroad. You obviously know much more about the Salt
March than I do.'

PIKE: Gandhi's 'March to the Sea' to protest the Salt Tax began at
Ahmedabad on March 12th. He reached the sea on the day
this letter was written.

FLORA: 'Nobody has mentioned it to me. If I remember I'll ask at
the Club tonight – I've had a visit from a clean young
Englishman who asked me to dinner. It was a bit of an
afterthought really. I think I made a gaffe by not announcing
myself to the Resident, and the young man, he was on a
horse, was sent to look me over. I think he ticked me off but
he was so nice it was hard to tell. I've a feeling I'm going to
have to stop in a minute. My artist is frowning at me and
then at the canvas as if one of us is misbehaving. He is
charming and eager and reminds me of Charlie Chaplin, not
the idiotic one in the films, the real one who was at the Trees'
lunch party.'

PIKE: It was Sir Herbert Beerbohm Tree who, soon after the
Crewe family arrived in London from Derbyshire, gave FC
her first employment, fleetingly as a cockney bystander in
the original production of *Pygmalion*, and, after objections
from Mrs Patrick Campbell, more permanently 'in the
office'. It was this connection which brought FC into the
orbit of Tree's daughter Iris and her friend Nancy Cunard,

33

and thence to the Sitwells, and arguably to the writing of
poetry.

FLORA: 'My poem, the one I'm not writing, is about sitting still
and being hot. It got defeated by its subject matter, and I
should be gone to the hills, I'm only waiting for my artist to
finish. The Hot Weather, they tell me, is about to start, but I
can't imagine anything hotter than this, and it will be
followed by the Wet Season, though I already feel as though
I'm sitting in a puddle. I don't think this is what Dr Guppy
meant by a warm climate.'

PIKE: Dr Alfred Guppy had been the Crewe family doctor since
the move from Derbyshire to London in 1913. His notes on
FC's illness, with reference to pulmonary congestion, are
first dated 1926.

FLORA: Oh, shut up!

(*It is as though she has turned on* PIKE. *Simultaneously,* DAS,
*losing his temper, is shouting in Hindi, 'Get off! Get off!' But
they are both shouting at a couple of unseen pi-dogs who have
been heard yapping and barking and are now fighting under the
verandah. In the middle of this,* DILIP *calls out for 'Eldon!'.
The fuss resolves itself.* PIKE *follows* DILIP *off. The dogs go
whining into oblivion.*)

DAS: Oh – fiddlesticks!

FLORA: I'm sorry – is it my fault?

DAS: No – how can it be?

FLORA: Is that so silly?

DAS: No . . . forgive me! Oh dear, Miss Crewe! Yesterday I felt
. . . a communion and today –

FLORA: Oh! . . . It *is* my fault! Yesterday I was writing a poem,
and today I have been writing a letter to my sister. That's
what it is.

DAS: A letter?

FLORA: I am not the same sitter. How thoughtless of me.

DAS: Yes. Yes.

FLORA: Are you angry ?

DAS: I don't know. Can we stop now? I would like a cigarette.
Would you care for a cigarette? They are Goldflake.

FLORA: No. But I'd like you to smoke.

34

DAS: Thank you. (*He lights a cigarette.*) You were writing to your sister? She is in England, of course.

FLORA: Yes, in London. Her name is Eleanor. She is much younger than me.

DAS: And also beautiful like you?

FLORA: Routine gallantry is disappointing from you.

DAS: (*Surprised*) Oh, it was not.

FLORA: Then, thank you.

DAS: Where does your sister live?

FLORA: That's almost the first thing you asked *me*. Would it mean anything to you?

(DAS *is loosening up again, regaining his normal good nature.*)

DAS: Oh, I have the whole of London spread out in my imagination. Challenge me, you will see!

FLORA: All right, she lives in Holborn.

DAS: (*Pause*) Oh. Which part of London is that?

FLORA: Well, it's – oh dear – between the Gray's Inn Road and –

DAS: Holl-born!

FLORA: Yes. Holborn.

DAS: But of course I know Holl-born! Charles Dickens lived in Doughty Street.

FLORA: Yes. Eleanor lives in Doughty Street.

DAS: But, Miss Crewe, *Oliver Twist* was written in that very street!

FLORA: Well, that's where Eleanor lives, over her work. She is the assistant to the editor of a weekly, *The Flag*.

DAS: *The Flag*!?

FLORA: You surely have never read that too?

DAS: No, but I have met the editor of *The Flag* –

FLORA: (*Realizing*) Yes – of course you have! That is how I came to be here. Mr Chamberlain gave me letters of introduction.

DAS: His lecture in Jummapur caused the Theosophical Society to be suspended for one year.

FLORA: I'm sorry. But it's not for me to apologize for the Raj.

DAS: Oh, it was not the Raj but the Rajah! His Highness is not a socialist! Do you agree with Mr Chamberlain's theory of Empire? I was not persuaded. Of course I am not an economist.

35

FLORA: That has never deterred Mr Chamberlain.

DAS: It is not my opinion that England's imperial adventure is simply to buy time against revolution at home.

FLORA: Political opinions are often, and perhaps entirely, a function of temperament, Mr Das. Eleanor and Mr Chamberlain are well suited.

DAS: Your sister shares Mr Chamberlain's opinions?

FLORA: Naturally.

DAS: Being his assistant, you mean.

FLORA: His mistress.

DAS: Oh.

FLORA: You should have been a barrister, Mr Das.

DAS: I am justly rebuked!

FLORA: It was not a rebuke. An unintended slight, perhaps.

DAS: I am very sorry about your sister. It must be a great sadness for you.

FLORA: I am very happy for her.

DAS: But she will never be married now! Unless Mr Chamberlain marries her.

FLORA: He is already married, otherwise he might.

DAS: Oh my goodness. How different things are. Here, you see, your sister would have been cast out – for bringing shame on her father's house.

(FLORA *snorts*.)

Yes – perhaps we are not so enlightened as you.

FLORA: Yes, perhaps. Well, you have had your cigarette. Are we going to continue?

DAS: No, not today.

FLORA: I'll go back to my poem.

DAS: There is no need.

FLORA: Well, I'll copy out my poem for my sister. I do that for safe keeping, you see. I'm sending her the drawing you did of me at the lecture.

DAS: (*Pause*) I have an appointment I had forgotten.

FLORA: Oh.

DAS: Actually you musn't feel obliged . . .

(*He begins gathering together his paraphernalia, apparently in a hurry now.*)

FLORA: What have I done?

DAS: Done? What should you have done?

FLORA: Stop it. Please. Stop being Indian.

DAS: (*Pause*) You have looked at the portrait, Miss Crewe?

FLORA: Oh, I see. Yes, yes . . . I did look.

DAS: Yes.

FLORA: I had a peep Why not? You wanted me to.

DAS: Yes, why not? You looked at the painting and you decided to spend the time writing letters. Why not?

FLORA: I'm sorry.

DAS: You still have said nothing about the painting.

FLORA: I know.

DAS: I cannot continue today.

FLORA: I understand. Will we try again tomorrow?

DAS: Tomorrow is Sunday.

FLORA: The next day.

DAS: Perhaps I cannot continue at all.

FLORA: Oh. And all because I said nothing. Are you at the mercy of every breeze that blows? Are you an artist at all?

DAS: Perhaps not! A mere sketcher – a hack painter who should be working in the bazaar!
(*He snatches up the 'pencil sketch' from under* FLORA's *hand.*)

FLORA: (*Realizing his intention*) Stop it!
(DAS *tears the paper in half.*)

DAS: Or in chalks on the ghat!

FLORA: Stop!
(*But* DAS *tears the paper again, and again and again, until it is in small pieces.*)
I'm ashamed of you!

DAS: Excuse me, please! I wish to leave. I will take the canvas –

FLORA: You will not!
(*It become a physical tussle. A struggle. She begins to gasp.*)

DAS: You need not see it again!

FLORA: You will not take anything! We will continue!

DAS: I do not want to continue, Miss Crewe. Please let go!

FLORA: I *won't* let you give up!

DAS: Let go, damn you, someone will see us!

FLORA: – and stop crying! You're not a baby!

37

DAS: (*Fighting her*) I will cry if I wish!

FLORA: Cry, then, but you will finish what you started! How else
will you ever . . . Oh!
(*And suddenly* FLORA *is helpless, gasping for breath.*)

DAS: Oh . . . oh, Miss Crewe – oh my God – let me help you. I'm
sorry. Please. Here, sit down –
(*She has had an attack of breathlessness. He helps her to a chair.*
FLORA *speaks with difficulty.*)

FLORA: Really, I'm all right.
(*Pause. She takes careful breaths.*) There.

DAS: What happened?

FLORA: I'm not allowed to wrestle with people. It's a considerable
nuisance. My lungs are bad, you see.

DAS: Let me move the cushion.

FLORA: It's all right. I'm back now. Panic over. I'm here for my
health, you see. Well, not *here* . . . I'll stay longer in the
Hills.

DAS: Yes, that will be better. You must go high.

FLORA: Yes. In a day or two.

DAS: What is the matter with you?

FLORA: Oh, sloshing about inside. Can't breathe under water.
I'm sorry if I frightened you.

DAS: You did frighten me.

FLORA: I'm soaking.

DAS: You must change your clothes.

FLORA: Yes. I'll go in now. I've got a shiver. Pull me up. Thank
you. Ugh. I need to be rubbed down like a horse.

DAS: Perhaps some tea . . . I'll go to the kitchen and tell –

FLORA: Yes. Would you? I'll have a shower and get into my
Wendy house.

DAS: Your . . .?

FLORA: My big towel is on the kitchen verandah – would you ask
Nazrul to put it in the bedroom?
(DAS *runs towards the kitchen verandah, shouting for Nazrul.*
FLORA *goes into the interior, into the bedroom, undressing as she
goes, dropping the blue dress on the floor, and enters the bathroom
in her underwear.*
DAS *returns, hurrying, with a white towel. He enters the interior*

38

cautiously, calling 'Miss Crewe . . .' He enters the bedroom and finds it empty. From the bathroom there is the sound of the water pipes thumping, but no sound of water.)

FLORA: (*Off stage*) Oh, damn, come on!

DAS: Miss Crewe . . .
(*The thumping in the pipes continues.*
DAS *approaches the bathroom door.*)

DAS: (*Louder*) Miss Crewe! I'm sorry, there's no –

FLORA: (*Off stage, shouts*) There's no water!
(*The thumping noise continues.*)

DAS: Miss Crewe! I'm sorry, the electricity –
(*The thumping noise suddenly stops.*)
(*In mid-shout*) The electric pump –

FLORA: (*Entering naked*) I have to lie down.

DAS: Oh! (*Thrusting the towel at her*) Oh, I'm so sorry!
(*Relieved of the towel,* DAS *is frozen with horror.*)

FLORA: I'm sorry, Mr Das, but really I feel too peculiar to mind at the moment.

DAS: (*Turning to leave hurriedly*) Please forgive me!

FLORA: No, please, there's water in the jug on the wash-stand.
(*She stands shivering, hugging the towel.*)
Do be quick.

DAS: (*Getting the water*) It's the electricity for the pump.

FLORA: Is there any water?

DAS: Yes, it's full . . . Here –
(*He gives her the jug, and turns away.*)

FLORA: Thank you. No, you do it. Over my head, and my back, please.
(DAS *pours the water over her, carefully.*)
Oh, heaven . . . Oh, thank you . . . I'm terribly sorry about this. Oh, that's good. Tip the last bit on the towel.

DAS: There . . .
(*She wipes her face with the wet corner of the towel . . .*)

FLORA: I feel as weak as a kitten.

DAS: I'm afraid that's all.

FLORA: Thank you.
(*She wraps the towel around herself.*) Could you do the net for me?

(DAS *lifts one side of the mosquito net and* FLORA *climbs onto the bed.*)

I'll be all right now.

DAS: (*Misunderstanding; leaving*) Yes, of course.

FLORA: Mr Das, I think there's soda water in the refrigerator. Would you . . .?

DAS: Oh yes. But is it locked? I cannot find Nazrul.

FLORA: Oh . . . I'm already hot again. And no electricity for the fan. It's too late for modesty. (*She discards the towel and gets under the sheet.*) Anyway, I'm your model.

DAS: I will fetch soda water from the shop.

FLORA: That was the thing I was going to ask you.

DAS: When?

FLORA: The delicate question . . . whether you would prefer to paint me nude.

DAS: Oh.

FLORA: I preferred it. I had more what-do-you-call it.

DAS: *Rasa.*

FLORA: (*Laughs quietly*) Yes, *rasa.*

(DAS *leaves the bedroom and goes along the verandah towards the servants' quarters and disappears round the corner.*

MRS SWAN *returns with Das's portrait of Flora. The canvas is inside a cardboard tube.*)

MRS SWAN: This is how it came back from the publishers. I tuck things away. You hold her and I'll pull the tube.

ANISH: Thank you.

MRS SWAN: Well, there she is.

ANISH: Oh . . .!

MRS SWAN: Yes, a bit much, isn't it?

ANISH: Oh . . . it's so vibrant.

MRS SWAN: Vibrant. Yes . . . oh, *you're* not going to blub too, are you?

ANISH: (*Weeping*) I'm sorry.

MRS SWAN: Don't worry. Borrow my hanky . . .

(*He takes her handkerchief.*)

ANISH: Please excuse me . . .

MRS SWAN: It just goes to show, you need an eye. And your father, after all, was, like you, an Indian painter.

ANISH: I'm sorry I . . . you know.

MRS SWAN: No, I should not have been disparaging. Let me see.
(*She takes the painting from* ANISH *and looks at it.*)
Yes, book jackets and biscuit tins are all very well, but
obviously there's something that stays behind in the painting
after all.

ANISH: Yes. Even unfinished.

MRS SWAN: Unfinished?

ANISH: It wasn't clear from the book, the way they cropped the
painting. You see where my father has only indicated the
tree, and the monkey . . . He would have gone back to
complete the background only when he considered the figure
finished. Believe me. I wondered why he hadn't signed it.
Now I know. My father abandoned this portrait.

MRS SWAN: Why?

ANISH: He began another one.

MRS SWAN: How do you know, Mr Das?

ANISH: Because I have it.
(*He opens his briefcase and withdraws the watercolour which is
hardly larger than the page of a book, protected by stiff boards.
He shows her the painting which is described in the text.*)

MRS SWAN: Oh heavens! Oh . . . yes . . . *of course.* How like
Flora.

ANISH: More than a good likeness, Mrs Swan.

MRS SWAN: No . . . I mean, *how like Flora!*
(*She continues to look at the painting.*
NAZRUL *returns to the dak bungalow, with shopping, the worse
for wear, disappearing towards the kitchen area where* DAS *starts
shouting at him and* NAZRUL *is heard protesting.*
DAS *returns to view with a bottle of soda-water. He speaks first
from outside the bedroom.*)

DAS: Nazrul has returned, most fortunately. I was able to unlock
the refrigerator. I have soda water.

FLORA: Thank you, Mr Das!
(DAS *enters the bedroom.*)

DAS: (*Approaching the bed*) Should I pour the water for you?
(*On the little table by the bed, outside the mosquito net, there is a
glass with a beaded lace cover.* DAS *pours the water.*)

Nazrul was delayed at the shops by a riot, he says. The police charged the mob with lathis, he could have easily been killed, but by heroism and inspired by his loyalty to the memsahib he managed to return only an hour late with all the food you gave him money for except two chickens which were torn from his grasp.

FLORA: Oh dear . . . you thanked him, I hope.

DAS: I struck him, of course. You should fine him for the chickens.

(FLORA *lifts the net sufficiently to take the glass from* DAS, *who then steps back rather further than necessary*.)

FLORA: (*Drinking*) Oh, that's nice. It's still cold. Perhaps there really was a riot.

DAS: Oh yes. Very probably. I have sent Nazrul to fetch the dhobi – you must have fresh linen for the bed. Nazrul will bring water but you must not drink it.

FLORA: Thank you.

(*The punkah begins to flap quite slowly, a regular beat*.)

DAS: I'm sure the electricity will return soon and the fan will be working.

FLORA: What's that? Oh, the punkah!

DAS: I have found a boy to be punkah-wallah.

FLORA: Yes, it makes a draught. Thank you. A *little* boy?

DAS: Don't worry about him. I've told him the memsahib is sick.

FLORA: The memsahib. Oh dear.

DAS: Yes, you are memsahib. Are you all right now, Miss Crewe?

FLORA: Oh yes. I'm only shamming now.

DAS: May I return later to make certain?

FLORA: Are you leaving now? Yes, I've made you late.

DAS: No, not at all. There is no one waiting for me. But the servant will return and . . . we Indians are frightful gossips, you see.

FLORA: Oh.

DAS: It is for yourself, not me.

FLORA: I don't believe you, Mr Das, not entirely.

DAS: To tell you the truth, this is the first time I have been alone in a room with an Englishwoman.

FLORA: Oh. Well, you certainly started at the deep end.

DAS: We need not refer to it again. It was a calamity.

FLORA: (*Amused*) A calamity! That's not spoken like an artist.

DAS: Then perhaps I am not an artist, as you said.

FLORA: I did not. All I did was hold my tongue and you had a tantrum. What would you have done in the rough and tumble of literary life in London? I expect you would have hanged yourself by now. When *Nymph in Her Orisons* came out one of the reviewers called it *Nymph In Her Mania*, as if my poems which I had found so hard to write were a kind of dalliance, no more than that. I met my critic somewhere a few months later and poured his drink over his head and went home and wrote a poem. So that was all right. But he'd taken weeks away from me and I mind that now.

DAS: Oh! – you're not dying are you?!

FLORA: I expect so, but I intend to take years and years about it. You'll be dead too, one day, so let me be a lesson to you. Learn to take no notice. I said nothing about your painting, if you want to know, because I thought you'd be an *Indian* artist.

DAS: An Indian artist?

FLORA: Yes. You *are* an Indian artist, aren't you? Stick up for yourself. Why do you like everything English?

DAS: I do not like everything English.

FLORA: Yes, you do. You're enthralled. Chelsea, Bloomsbury, Oliver Twist, Goldflake cigarettes, Winsor and Newton . . . even painting in oils, that's not Indian. You're trying to paint me from my point of view instead of yours – what you *think* is my point of view. You *deserve* the bloody Empire!

DAS: (*Sharply*) May I sit down please?

FLORA: Yes, do. Flora is herself again.

DAS: I will move the chair near the door.

FLORA: You can move the chair onto the verandah if you like, so the servants won't –

DAS: I would like to smoke, that is what I meant.

FLORA: Oh. I'm sorry. Thank you. In that case, can you see me through the net from over there?

DAS: Barely.

FLORA: Is that no or yes?

(*She raises the sheet off her body and flaps it like a sail and lets it settle again.*)

Oof! – that's better! That's what I love about my little house – you can see out better than you can see in.

DAS: (*Passionately*) But you are looking at such a house! The bloody Empire finished off Indian painting!

(*Pause.*)

Excuse me.

FLORA: No, that's better.

DAS: Perhaps your sister is right. And Mr Chamberlain. Perhaps we have been robbed. Yes; when the books are balanced. The women here wear saris made in Lancashire. The cotton is Indian but we cannot compete in the weaving. Mr Chamberlain explained it all to us in simple Marxist language. Actually, he caused some offence. He didn't realize we had Marxists of our own, many of them in the Jummapur Theosophical Society.

FLORA: Mr Coomaraswami . . .?

DAS: No, not Mr Coomaraswami. *His* criticism is that you haven't exploited India *enough*. 'Where are the cotton mills? The steel mills? No investment, no planning. The Empire has failed us!' That is Mr Coomaraswami. Well, the Empire will one day be gone like the Mughal Empire before it, and only their monuments remain – the visions of Shah Jahan! – of Sir Edwin Lutyens!

FLORA: 'Look on my works, ye mighty, and despair!'

DAS: (*Delighted*) Oh yes! Finally like the empire of Ozymandias! Entirely forgotten except in a poem by an English poet. You see how privileged we are, Miss Crewe. Only in art can empires cheat oblivion, because only the artist can say, 'Look on my works, ye mighty, and despair!'

FLORA: I just didn't like you thinking English was better because it was English. Can't you paint me without thinking of Rossetti or Millais? Especially without thinking of Holman Hunt. Did you consider my question?

DAS: When you stood . . . with the pitcher of water, you were an Alma-Tadema.

FLORA: Well, I don't want to be painted like that either.

44

DAS: I don't understand why you are angry with me.

FLORA: You were painting me as a gift, to please me.

DAS: Yes. Yes, it was a gift for you.

FLORA: If you don't start learning to *take* you'll never be shot of us. *Who whom*. Nothing else counts. Mr Chamberlain is bosh. Mr Coomaraswami is bosh. It's your country, and we've got it. Everything else is bosh. When I was Modi's model I might as well have *been* a table. When he was done, he got rid of me. There was no question who whom. You'd never change his colour on a map. But please light your Goldflake.

(*Pause.* DAS *lights his cigarette with a match.*)

DAS: I like the Pre-Raphaelites because they tell stories. That is my tradition, too. I am Rajasthani. Our art is narrative art, stories from the legends and romances. The English painters had the Bible and Shakespeare, King Arthur . . . We had the Bhagavata Purana, and the Rasikpriya which was written exactly when Shakespeare had his first play. And long before Chaucer we had the Chaurapanchasika, from Kashmir, which is poems of love written by the poet of the court on his way to his execution for falling in love with the king's daughter, and the king liked the poems so very much he pardoned the poet and allowed the lovers to marry.

FLORA: Oh . . .

DAS: But the favourite book of the Rajput painters was the Gita Govinda which tells the story of Krishna and Radha the most beautiful of the herdswomen.

(*The ceiling fan starts working.*)

FLORA: The electricity is on.

DAS: You will be a little cooler now.

FLORA: Yes. I might have a sleep.

DAS: That would be good.

FLORA: Mr Durance has invited me to dinner at the Club.

DAS: Will you be well enough?

FLORA: I am well now.

DAS: That is good. Goodbye, then.

FLORA: Were Krishna and Radha punished in the story?

DAS: What for?

FLORA: I should have come here years ago. The punkah boy can stop now. Will you give him a rupee? I'll return it tomorrow.

DAS: I will give him an anna. A rupee would upset the market.

(DAS *leaves*.

FLORA *remains in the bed*.)

ACT TWO

The Jummapur Club after sundown. Gramophone music. Three couples are dancing: FLORA *and* DURANCE, *the* RESIDENT *and the* ENGLISHWOMAN, *and a third couple, an* ENGLISHMAN *and* ENGLISH LADY.

Somewhat removed from the dance floor is a verandah, which is spacious enough not only for the necessary furniture but also for two gymnasium horses, fitted out with stirrups and reins. These 'horses' are used for practising polo swings and there are indeed a couple of polo sticks, a couple of topees and odd bits of gear lying in the corner.

PIKE *is sitting alone on the verandah. He is tieless, wearing a Lacoste-type short-sleeved sports shirt.*

ENGLISHWOMAN: Are you writing a poem about India, Flora?

FLORA: Trying to!

ENGLISHMAN: Kipling – there's a poet! 'Though I've belted you and flayed you, by the living Gawd that made you, you're a better man than I am Gunga Din!'

ENGLISHWOMAN: Gerald, you're showing us up. Flora writes *modern* poetry, don't you, dear, not the sort people can *remember*.

FLORA: Oh, but I like all kinds.

RESIDENT: The only poet I *know* is Alfred Housman. I expect you've come across him.

FLORA: (*Pleased*) Oh yes, indeed I have!

RESIDENT: A dry old stick, isn't he?

FLORA: Oh – come *across him* –

RESIDENT: He hauled me though 'Ars Amatoria' when I was up at Trinity.

FLORA: (*Pleased*) Oh, yes – the Art of Love!

RESIDENT: When it comes to love, Housman said, you're either an Ovid man or a Virgil man – *omnia vincit amor et nos cedamus amori* – you can't win against love; we give in to it. That's Virgil. Housman was an Ovid man – *et mihi cedet amor* – 'Love won't win against me!'

47

FLORA: I'm a Virgil man.

RESIDENT: Are you? Well, you make friends more quickly that way.

ENGLISHWOMAN: Will you be here for the Queen's Ball, Flora?

FLORA: The . . . ?

ENGLISHWOMAN: It comes off next month, Queen Victoria's birthday, and there's the gymkhana!

FLORA: Oh . . . I can't, I'm afraid. I'll be going up the country soon; is that the expression?

RESIDENT: Of course, you're here on doctor's orders, I believe.

FLORA: Why . . . yes . . .

RESIDENT: If there's anything you need or want you tell David – right, David?

DURANCE: Yes, sir.

FLORA: Thank you. He's already promised me a go in the Daimler.

DURANCE: (*Embarrassed*) Oh . . . Flora's keen on autos.

ENGLISHWOMAN: If you like cars, His Highness has got about eighty-six of them. Collects them like stamps.

FLORA: His Highness?

ENGLISHMAN: The Rajah of Jummapur. The collectingness is terrific.

(*Another record begins to play*.)

RESIDENT: Well, don't let us stop you enjoying yourselves.

DURANCE: Would you like to dance, Flora?

FLORA: I'm out of puff. Do you think there might be more air outside?

DURANCE: On the verandah? Any air that's going. Should we take a peg with us?

(. . .*The Kipling fan, unseen, is singing*:)

ENGLISHMAN: 'On the road to Mandalay

Where the flyin' fishes play,

An' the dawn come up like thunder outer China crost the Bay!'

(*The dancers disperse.*

DILIP, *now smartly dressed in a jacket and tie, enters the verandah from within, in something of a hurry, carrying a jacket and a tie. The jacket is a faded beige gabardine with metal*

48

buttons, the skimpy jacket of a servant. On the breast, however,
not instantly apparent, is a short strip of grimy campaign
ribbons.)

DILIP: Here I am at last! – I am so sorry, my fault entirely for not
thinking to mention – but, look – all will be well in a jiffy! –
and I have terrifically good news.

PIKE: (*Getting up*) Thank you, Dilip – what . . .?

DILIP: (*Helping him on with the jacket, which is too small for* PIKE)
Put it on and I will tell you. The jacket is a miserable
garment, and our benefactor, I'm afraid, isn't quite your
size.

PIKE: (*Implausibly*) This is fine.

DILIP: The tie, on the other hand, is tip-top, Jummapur Cricket
Club. My friend Mr Balvinder Lal keeps a small stock on the
premises. I spared you the blazer.
(PIKE *obligingly starts putting on the striped tie.*)

PIKE: Do you mean you can't come in here without a jacket and
tie, not ever?

DILIP: Not in the dining-room after sunset. Oh these rules are
absurd! But – Eldon – something wonderful has come of it. I
have discovered the name of your painter!

PIKE: You *have*?

DILIP: I have! His name was Nirad Das. Now we can *research*!

PIKE: But Dilip – but that's – how did you – ?

DILIP: It was God. If you had been wearing a jacket we would still
be in the dark. But in borrowing the jacket, you see – oh,
don't think that I discuss your affairs – it only seemed, shall I
say, tactical to point out your distinction –

PIKE: Dilip, never mind about that –

DILIP: Nor, for that matter, was the owner of the jacket indulging
in impertinent curiosity about your private business, I assure
you – actually, I know him well, he is an Old Soldier,
formerly in the 6th Rajputana Rifles –

PIKE: Dilip – *please*!

DILIP: He remembers the English lady who stayed in the dak
house.

PIKE: Who remembers?

DILIP: The owner of this jacket.

49

PIKE: He . . . he *remembers* . . .? But are you sure it was the same – ?

DILIP: Oh yes – he saw Miss Crewe having her portrait painted.

PIKE: (*When he recovers*) I have to talk to him.

DILIP: Of course. After dinner we will –

PIKE: *After dinner?* He could *die* while I'm eating! Where is he? Ask him to have dinner with us.

DILIP: Oh, that is not possible, you see.

PIKE: Why not?

DILIP: He would not like that. Anyway, he does not have a jacket.

PIKE: We're getting off the point there –

DILIP: Also, he is working now.

PIKE: What, he works here?

DILIP: Exactly. He works here. He is in charge of supervising the cloakroom.

PIKE: Well, that's wonderful. Show me the way.

DILIP: Eldon, please be guided by me. We will not rush at the fences in the lavatory.

(DILIP *points at the ribbons on* PIKE'*s breast.*)

One of these is the ribbon for '39 to '45. This one, I think, is the Burma Star. He is without one leg. He has no sons. He has three daughters, two of them unmarried and to marry the third he sold his army pension and secured for himself a job which is cleaning toilets. Tomorrow there is time, there is reflection, there is . . . esteem . . . We can take a cup of tea together on the *maidan* and talk of old times. Believe me.

PIKE: Esteem. If he dies I'll kill you.

DILIP: (*Laughs*) He will not die. Let me go and see if our table's ready. Oh, how terrible – ! with all this excitement I have not offered you an aperitif.

PIKE: What's his name, Dilip?

DILIP: Mr Ram Sunil Singh, formerly Subadar, B Company, 6th Rajputana Rifles.

PIKE: He must be pretty ancient.

(*The gramophone music creeps back in.* FLORA, *alone, comes out onto the verandah.*)

DILIP: No, not at all. He was only a small boy, you see. One day

the Memsahib was sick and Ram Sunil Singh worked the
punkah to cool the air. Mr Nirad Das gave him two annas.
One does not forget such things. (*Leaving now.*) I won't be a
jiff. I must say, I could eat a horse!
(DILIP *leaves.*)

FLORA: 'My suitor – I suppose I must call him that, though I
swear I've done nothing to encourage him – came to fetch me
in an open Daimler which drew such a crowd, and off we
went with people practically falling off the mud-guards,
rather like leaving Bow Street – my God, how strange, that
was ten years ago almost to the day.'

PIKE: In fact, nine. See 'The Woman Who Wrote What She
Knew', E. C. Pike, *Modern Language Review*, Spring 1979.

FLORA: 'And everyone at the Club was very friendly, going out of
their way to explain that although they didn't go in much for
poetry, they had nothing against it, so that was all right, and
dinner was soup, boiled fish, lamb cutlets, sherry trifle and
sardines on toast, and it beats me how we're getting away
with it, darling, I wouldn't trust some of them to run the
Hackney Empire. Well, it's all going to end. That's official. I
heard it from the horse's mouth –'
(*The* RESIDENT *and the* ENGLISHWOMAN *dance into view, in a
cheerful mood.*)

RESIDENT: (*Dancing*) (a) It is our moral duty to remain and (b) we
will shirk it.
(*The* RESIDENT *and the* ENGLISHWOMAN, *dancing, spin out of
view.*
DURANCE *appears now, followed by a* SERVANT *with two
tumblers of whisky and a soda syphon on a salver.*)

DURANCE: Here we are. Two burra-pegs.

FLORA: Lots of soda with mine, please.

DURANCE: I'll do it.
(*The* SERVANT *bows and leaves.*
DILIP *reappears.*)

DILIP: Eldon! We can eat! I hope you will like my Club. The
Jummapur Palace is a beautiful hotel, naturally, but *this* was
the place in the old days when the palace was still the private
residence of the rajah.

PIKE: (*Following him out*) Where does he live now?

DILIP: (*Leaving*) In the penthouse! The fish curry is usually good, and on no account miss the bread-and-butter pudding!

DURANCE: Say when.

(DURANCE *deals with the drinks*.)

FLORA: When . . . Cheers.

DURANCE: Cheers.

FLORA: I'm sorry I packed up on you.

DURANCE: This is nicer. So you've come to India for your health . . .

FLORA: Is that amusing?

DURANCE: Well, it is rather. Have you seen the English cemetery?

FLORA: No.

DURANCE: I must take you there.

FLORA: Oh.

DURANCE: People here drop like flies – cholera, typhoid, malaria – men, women and children, here one day, gone the next. Are you sure the doctor said India?

FLORA: He didn't say India. He said a sea voyage and somewhere warm. I wanted to come to India.

DURANCE: Good for you. Live dangerously. In a month, you can't imagine it, the heat. But you'll be gone to the hills, so you'll be all right. (*Referring to the chair*) There we are. Long-sleever. Good for putting the feet up.

FLORA: Yes – long-sleever. Thank you. It's a nice Club.

DURANCE: Yes, it's decent enough. There are not so many British here so we tend to mix more.

FLORA: With the Indians?

DURANCE: No. In India proper, I mean *our* India, there'd be two or three Clubs. The box-wallahs would have their own and the government people would stick together, you know how it is – and the Army . . .

FLORA: Mr Das called you Captain.

DURANCE: Yes, I'm Army. Seconded, of course. There are two of us Juniors – political agents we call ourselves when we're on tour round the States. Jummapur is not one of your twenty-one-gun salute states, you see – my Chief is in charge of half a dozen native states.

FLORA: In charge?

DURANCE: Oh yes.

FLORA: Is he Army? No – how silly –

DURANCE: He's Indian Civil Service. The heaven-born. A
Brahmin.

FLORA: Not seriously?

DURANCE: Yes, seriously. Oh no, not a Brahmin seriously. But it
might come to that with I-zation.

FLORA: . . .?

DURANCE: Indianization. It's all over, you know. We have Indian
officers in the Regiment now. My fellow Junior here is
Indian, too, terribly nice chap – he's ICS, passed the exam,
did his year at Cambridge, learned polo and knives-and-
forks, and here he is, a pukkah sahib in the Indian Civil
Service.

FLORA: Is he here?

DURANCE: At the Club? No, he can't come into the Club.

FLORA: Oh.

DURANCE: Cheers. Your health, Flora. I drink to your health, for
which you came. I wish you were staying longer. I mean,
only for my sake, Flora.

FLORA: Yes, but I'm not. So that's that. Don't look hangdog.
You might like me less and less as you got to know me.

DURANCE: Will you come riding in the morning?

FLORA: Seriously.

DURANCE: Yes, seriously. Will you?

FLORA: In the Daimler?

DURANCE: No. Say you will. We'll have to go inside in a minute if
no one comes out.

FLORA: Why?

DURANCE: There's nothing to do here except gossip, you see.
They're all agog about you. One of the wives claims . . .
Were you in the papers at home? Some scandal about one of
your books, something like that?

FLORA: I can see why you're nervous, being trapped out here with
me – let's go in –

DURANCE: No – I'm sorry. Flora . . .? Pax? Please.

FLORA: All right, Pax.

(*He kisses her, uninvited, tentatively.*)

DURANCE: Sealed with a kiss.

FLORA: No more. I mean it, David. Think of your career.

DURANCE: Are you really a scandalous woman?

FLORA: I was for a while. I was up in court, you know. Bow Street.

DURANCE: (*Alarmed*) Oh, not really?

FLORA: Almost really. I was a witness. The publisher was in the dock, but it was my poems – my first book.

DURANCE: Oh, I say.

FLORA: The case was dismissed on a technicality, and the policemen were awfully sweet, they got me away through the crowd in a van. My sister was asked to leave school. But that was mostly my own fault – the magistrate asked me why all the poems seemed to be about sex, and I said. 'Write what you know' – just showing off. I was practically a virgin, but it got me so thoroughly into the newspapers my name rings a bell even with the wife of a bloody jute planter or something in the middle of Rajputana, damn, damn, damn, no, let's go inside.

DURANCE: Sit down, that's an order.

(DURANCE, *who has been standing, swings himself aboard one of the gymnasium horses.*)

FLORA: Oh dear, you're not going to be masterful, are you?

DURANCE: (*Laughs*) Do you like polo?

FLORA: Well, I don't play a lot.

DURANCE: Measure your swing, you see . . .

(*He swings the polo mallet.*)

How's your whisky?

FLORA: Excellent. All the better for being forbidden. My God, where did that moon come from?

DURANCE: Better. I love this country, don't you?

FLORA: What's going to happen to it? The riot in town this morning . . . does that happen often?

DURANCE: Not here, no. The jails are filling up in British India.

FLORA: Well, then.

DURANCE: It wasn't against us, it was Hindu and Moslem. Gandhi's salt march reached the sea today, did you hear?

54

FLORA: No. I want to know.

DURANCE: Our Congress Hindus closed their shops in sympathy, and the Moslems wouldn't join in, that's all it was about.

FLORA: My cook came home minus two chickens.

DURANCE: The Indian National Congress is all very well, but to the Moslems, Congress means Gandhi . . . a Hindu party in all but name.

FLORA: Will Gandhi be arrested?

DURANCE: No, no. The salt tax is a lot of nonsense actually. It works out at about four annas a year. Most Indians didn't even know there *was* a salt tax.

FLORA: Well, they do now.

DURANCE: Yes. They do now.

FLORA: Let me have a go.

(*There is a solar topee on the second horse. She puts the topee on her head, and puts her foot in the stirrup.* DURANCE, *laughing, helps* FLORA *to heave herself on board the second horse.*)

Oh yes, nothing to it. Yes, I can see the point of this, what fun, polo and knives-and-forks. Is that all you need to govern India?

DURANCE: (*Laughs*) Oh yes. There's about four of our chaps for every million Indians.

FLORA: Why do the Indians let us?

DURANCE: Why not? We're better at it.

FLORA: Are we?

DURANCE: Ask them.

FLORA: Who?

DURANCE: The natives. Ask them. We've pulled this country together. It's taken a couple of hundred years with a hiccup or two but the place now works.

FLORA: That's what you love, then? What you created?

DURANCE: Oh no – it's India I love. I'll show you.

(*The horses whinny.* FLORA's *horse lurches just enough to almost throw her. She squeals, quite happily.*)

(*The scene becomes exterior. The actors remain astride the gym horses.*
Ground mist.

The horses whinny, the riders shift and rebalance themselves,
FLORA *whooping with alarm, and birds are crying out,*
distancing rapidly.)

DURANCE: Sand grouse! Are you all right?

FLORA: They startled me.

DURANCE: Time to trot.

FLORA: Oops – David – I'll have to tell you – stop! It's my first
time on a horse, you see.

DURANCE: Yes, I could tell.

FLORA: (*Miffed*) Could you? Even walking? I felt so proud when
we were walking.

DURANCE: No, no good, I'm afraid.

FLORA: Oh, damn you. I'm going to get off.

DURANCE: No, no, just sit. He's a chair. Breathe in. India smells
wonderful, doesn't it?

FLORA: Out here it does.

DURANCE: You should smell chapattis cooking on a camel-dung
fire out in the Thar Desert. Perfume!

FLORA: What were you doing out there?

DURANCE: Cooking chapattis on a camel-dung fire. (*Laughs*) I'll
tell you where it all went wrong with us and India. It was the
Suez Canal. It let the women in.

FLORA: Oh!

DURANCE: Absolutely. When you had to sail round the Cape this
was a man's country and we mucked in with the natives. The
memsahibs put a stop to that. The memsahib won't muck in,
won't even be alone in a room with an Indian.

FLORA: Oh . . .

DURANCE: Don't point your toes out. May I ask you a personal
question?

FLORA: No.

DURANCE: All right.

FLORA: I wanted to ask *you* something. How did the Resident
know I came to India for my health?

DURANCE: It's his business to know. Shoulders back. Reins too
slack.

FLORA: But I didn't tell anybody.

DURANCE: Obviously you did.

FLORA: Only Mr Das.

DURANCE: Oh well, there you are. Jolly friendly of you, of course, sharing a confidence, lemonade, all that, but they can't help themselves bragging about it.

FLORA: (*Furious*) Rubbish!

DURANCE: Well . . . I stand corrected.

FLORA: I'm sorry. I don't believe you, though.

DURANCE: Righto.

FLORA: I'm sorry. Pax.

DURANCE: Flora.

FLORA: No.

DURANCE: Would you marry me?

FLORA: No.

durance: Would you think about it?

FLORA: No. Thank you.

DURANCE: Love at first sight, you see. Forgive me.

FLORA: Oh, David.

DURANCE: Knees together.

FLORA: 'Fraid so.

(*She laughs without malice but unrestrainedly. The horses trot.*)

(DILIP *and* PIKE *are in the garden/courtyard of the Jummapur Palace Hotel, which was formerly the Palace of the Rajah of Jummapur. They are brought drinks – reassuringly American cola – served by a* WAITER *decked out in the authentic livery of the old regime.*

Thus, the SERVANTS *operate freely between the two periods.*)

DILIP: Poor Mr Nirad Das! Six months in the choky for throwing a mango!

PIKE: It's wonderful, Dilip. Subadar Ram Sunil Singh the toilet cleaner is a goldmine!

DILIP: And he thinks you are one! How satisfactory.

PIKE: Did I give him too much? The poverty here is so . . . Like the beggars at the traffic lights . . . I started off shoving rupees, you know, through the window . . . But it gets impossible. You can't . . . there's more of them then you can ever . . . I mean there's nothing to be in between, you have to be St Francis or some rich bastard who ignores them, there's

57

nothing between that can touch it, the problem. Not St Francis, I didn't mean any disrespect, they're not *birds* – but Mother Teresa, some kind of saint. I lock the doors now. That's the truth. First thing I do now when the taxi hits a red light, I check the doors, wind up the window. But this one, she had this baby at the breast, I mean she looked *sixty*, and – well, this is the thing, she had a stump, you see, she had no hand, just this stump, up against the glass, and it was . . . raw . . . so when the light changed, the stump left this . . . smear . . .

DILIP: You have to understand that begging is a profession. Like dentistry. Like shining shoes. It's a service. Every so often, you need to get a tooth filled, or your shoes shined, or to give alms. So when a beggar presents himself to you, you have to ask yourself – do I need a beggar today? If you do, give him alms. If you don't, don't. You have beggars in America.

PIKE: We have bums, winos, people down on their luck . . . it's not a *service*, for God's sake.

DILIP: Ah well, we are in a higher stage of development.

PIKE: Is that Hinduism, Dilip?

DILIP: (*Kindly*) It was a witticism, Eldon.

PIKE: Oh . . . right.

DILIP: One can see why the Theosophical Society transplanted itself from America. (*With his drink*) Let's drink to Madame Blavatsky.

PIKE: Who's she?

DILIP: What? Don't you know 'Bagpipe Music'?

PIKE: Oh . . . (yeah).

DILIP: 'It's no go the yogi man, it's no go Blavatsky . . .'

PIKE: MacNeice, right.

DILIP: Madame Blavatsky was a famous name in India, she *was* the Theosophical Society. Of course, she was long dead by 1930, and now long forgotten, except in my favourite poem in the Oxford Book of English Verse.

PIKE: Why are you so crazy about English, Dilip?

DILIP: I'm not!

PIKE: You love it!

DILIP: Yes, I do. I love it.

PIKE: Yes. You do.

DILIP: (*Cheerfully*) Yes, it's a disaster for us! Fifty years of Independence and we are still hypnotized! Jackets and ties must be worn! English-model public schools for the children of the elite, and the voice of Bush House is heard in the land. Gandhi would fast again, I think. Only, this time he'd die. It was not for this India, I think, that your Nirad Das and his friends held up their home-made banner at the Empire Day gymkhana. It was not for this that he threw his mango at the Resident's car. What a pity, though, that all his revolutionary spirit went into his life and none into his art.

PIKE: Do you think he had a relationship with Flora Crewe?

DILIP: But of course – a portrait is a relationship.

PIKE: No, a *relationship*.

DILIP: I don't understand you.

PIKE: He painted her nude.

DILIP: I don't think so.

PIKE: Somebody did.

DILIP: In 1930, an Englishwoman, an Indian painter . . . it is out of the question.

PIKE: Not if they had a relationship.

DILIP: Oh . . . a *relationship*? Is that what you say? (*Amused*) A relationship!

PIKE: This is serious.

DILIP: (*Laughing*) Oh, it's very serious. What do you say for – well, for 'relationship'?

PIKE: Buddies.

(DILIP *almost falls off his chair with merriment*.)

Please, Dilip . . .

DILIP: (*Recovering*) Well, we will never know. You are constructing an edifice of speculation on a smudge of paint on paper, which no longer exists.

PIKE: It must exist – look how far I've come to find it.

DILIP: Oh, very Indian! Well, if so, there are two ways to proceed. First, you can go around Jummapur looking at every piece of paper you come to. Second, you can stand in one place and look at every piece of paper that comes to you.

(*A* WAITER *brings a note to* PIKE, *and leaves*.)

PIKE: (*Reading the note*) He's coming down. I thought maybe he'd ask us up to the penthouse.

DILIP: Don't be offended.

PIKE: I'm not offended.

DILIP: He is not the Rajah now, he is an ordinary politician. He has your letter. I hope he can help you. In any case, it is better if I leave you so he does not need to wear two hats.

PIKE: What do I call him?

DILIP: Your Highness. He will correct you.

(DILIP *leaves.*

FLORA *enters, dressed for tiffin with his Highness the Rajah of Jummapur.*)

FLORA: 'I was let off church parade, being a suspected Bolshie, and I was writing on my verandah after my early-morning ride when what should turn up but a Rolls Royce circa 1912 but brand new, as it were, with a note from his Highness the Rajah of Jummapur going on about my spiritual beauty and inviting me to tiffin.'

RAJAH: (*Entering*) The spiritual beauty of Jummapur has been increased a thousandfold by your presence, Miss Crewe!

FLORA: 'Well, what is a poor girl to do? Hop into the back of the Rolls, that's what.'

(*The* RAJAH *shakes hands with* FLORA *who has stood up.*)

RAJAH: How delightful that you were able to come! I understand you are a connoisseur of the automobile.

FLORA: Oh, how sweet of you to ask me . . . your Highness.

RAJAH: Unfortunately I cannot show them all at once because I have many more motor cars than mechanics, of course. But we can sit and chat between the scenes.

FLORA: I would be happy to walk around them, your Highness.

RAJAH: Oh, but that would deny them their spiritual essence. They would not be automobiles if we did the moving and they did the sitting.

(*A stately* concours d'elegance *of motor cars, as distinguished as they are invisible, begins to pass in front of them.*)

FLORA: Oh – ! What a beauty! A Duesenberg! And what's that? – Oh, my goodness, it's a Type 41 Bugatti! I've never seen one! And a . . . is it an Isotta-Fraschini?

RAJAH: Possibly. I acquired it by way of settlement of a gambling debt at Bendor Westminster's. Do you know him?

FLORA: I don't know any dukes.

RAJAH: He's my neighbour in the South of France. I go to the South of France every year, you see, for my health. (*He laughs.*) But *you* have come to India for your health!

FLORA: (*Not pleased*) Well . . . yes, Your Highness. Everybody seems to know everything about me.

RAJAH: Mr Churchill was in Bendor's house party. He paints. Like your friend Mr Das. Do you know Mr Churchill?

FLORA: Not very well.

RAJAH: I was at school with him, apparently. I can't remember him at all. But I read Mr Churchill's speeches with great interest, and . . . oh – look at that one! I couldn't resist the headlamps. So enormous, like the eggs of a chromium bird.

FLORA: Yes – a Brancusi!

RAJAH: You know them all, Miss Crewe! . . . Yes, Mr Churchill is perfectly right, don't you agree, Miss Crewe?

FLORA: About what exactly, Your Highness?

RAJAH: In his own words, the loss of India would reduce Britain to a minor power.

FLORA: That may be, but one must consider India's interests, too.

RAJAH: I must consider Jummapur's interests.

FLORA: Yes, of course, but aren't they the same thing?

RAJAH: No, no. Independence would be the beginning of the end for the Princely States. Though in a sense you are right, too – Independence will be the end of the unity of the Subcontinent. Look at the hullabaloo in the town yesterday. You tell Mr Churchill from me, Miss Crewe. My grandfather stood firm with the British during the First Uprising.

FLORA: The . . .?

RAJAH: In 1857 the danger was from fundamentalists –

FLORA: The Mutiny . . .

RAJAH: – today it is the progressives. No offence, Miss Crewe!

FLORA: I take it as a compliment.

RAJAH: Marxism. Civil disobedience. But I told the Viceroy, you have to fight them the same way, you won't win by playing cricket.

(*There is a pause in the cavalcade of motor cars. A* SERVANT *appears with a tray of drinks, fruit, a cigarette box, finger bowls and napkins.*)

Ah, the first interval. Do you smoke? No? I enjoy a cigarette. You must tell me when you have had enough of automobiles. There are one or two things in my apartments which have drawn favourable comment from historians of Indian art, even exclamations of delight if I may be honest with you. Do you enjoy art, Miss Crewe?

FLORA: Frequently.

RAJAH: But of course you do, you are a poet. I would be happy to show you.

FLORA: I would like that very much.

RAJAH: You would really? Yes, I can see you are a true seeker. My ancestors' atelier produced some work which in my opinion compares with the best workshops of Rajasthan.

FLORA: I would like to see *everything*!

RAJAH: So you shall. Well, not quite everything, perhaps. Some of the most exquisite work, alas, is considered indelicate.

FLORA: Considered by whom? By you?

RAJAH: Oh no. In my culture, you see, erotic art has a long history and a most serious purpose.

FLORA: (*Unangrily*) But only for men, your Highness?

RAJAH: I have made you angry. I am terribly sorry. I should not have mentioned it.

FLORA: I'm very glad you did. Otherwise I should not have seen it.

RAJAH: (*Comfortably*) Oh, my dear Miss Crewe, you are making me uncomfortable! What can I say?

FLORA: What do you usually say, Your Highness? Well . . . here are some more cars . . . I'm going to leave it to you.

(*Another car purrs by in front of them.*)

(*Pleased*) Oh – a Silver Ghost. Goodness, that's beautiful.

RAJAH: Will you not have some fruit, Miss Crewe?

FLORA: Yes, I think I might. Thank you.

(From the tray, which is piled up with tangerines, bananas, lychees, etc., she takes an apricot. She bites into it.)
Apricot is my favourite word.

RAJAH: Miss Crewe, you shall see all the paintings you wish to see; on the condition that you allow me to choose one to present to you.

FLORA: Oh . . . thank you, Your Highness, but if there are going to be conditions, I'm not sure I want to see *any*.

RAJAH: The English ladies came, Mrs Tuke, Mrs Stokely-Smith, Mrs Blane . . . a dozen of them, to see the lily pools, the flower garden . . . They drank tea with me and I offered them fruit, but they would only eat the fruit which had a skin they could remove, you see.

FLORA: Yes, I see. Then I accept.
(The next car has a distinct musical horn, which makes FLORA gasp and almost jump out of her chair.)
Oh! – I *know* that one!

RAJAH: Of course you do, Miss Crewe!

FLORA: No, I really know it. Where did you get it?

RAJAH: Well . . . from a car shop.

FLORA: Could you make him stop a moment.
(FLORA stands up. The RAJAH signals for the car to stop and it does so, idling. FLORA takes a step or two towards the unseen car.)

FLORA: 'And oh my darling, it was Gus's Bentley! I mean it was absolutely the one I broke my engagement in when I took Gus to the French paintings at Heals – it still had the A B number-plate!'

RAJAH: It has memories for you, Miss Crewe?

FLORA: Yes, it does. Can I go and sit in it?

RAJAH: Romantic memories?

FLORA: The Tottenham Court Road, ten years ago. I hit a man with my shoe in that car.
(FLORA, going to the car, leaves the stage.)

PIKE: Augustus de Boucheron enjoyed brief celebrity as a millionaire philanthropist and patron of the arts. FC met him – and received his proposal of marriage – on December 3rd 1917. The occasion was Modigliani's first show, in Paris. FC

sat for the artist soon afterwards. At the exhibition of
Modern French Art at Heal and Sons in the Tottenham
Court Road, London, in August 1919, Modigliani was one of
several newer artists shown with the better known Matisse,
Picasso and Derain. FC arrived at Heals with de Boucheron,
expecting to see her portrait, but before they got out of the
Bentley she discovered that her fiancé had bought the
painting from the artist and, as he triumphantly confessed,
taken it back to the Ritz Hotel and burned it in a bathtub. In
the ensuing row, FC returned de Boucheron's engagement
ring, and made plans to sit for Modigliani again in the
autumn of that year. But she delayed, arriving in Paris only
on the morning of January 23rd, unaware that Modigliani
had been taken to hospital. He died on the following
evening, without regaining consciousness, of tuberculosis,
aged thirty-five. De Boucheron, under his real name Perkins
Butcher, went to prison in 1925 for issuing a false prospectus.
His end is unknown.

(The RAJAH *looks around the courtyard seeking someone . . . and
spots* PIKE. PIKE *has not noticed him. The* RAJAH, *soi disant,
approaches* PIKE.)

RAJAH: Professor Pike . . . ?

PIKE: (*Jumping up*) Oh! – indeed, yes – thank you.

RAJAH: (*Shaking hands*) How do you do?

PIKE: An honour, sir.

RAJAH: (*Waving* PIKE *back into his chair*) Please . . . I'm so sorry
to have kept you waiting. But what I say is, a punctual
politician is a politician who does not have enough to do. In
other words, an impossibility.

PIKE: I'm so grateful to you for this.

RAJAH: No, no – delighted. I hope you find the hotel
comfortable? We are not one of the international chains, you
know. You mustn't be deluded on that point, no matter how
much we exert ourselves to delude you.

PIKE: The hotel is excellent, your Highness.

RAJAH: Actually, I am not 'Your Highness', I am, in fact, just one
of 542 members of the Lok Sabha, the House of the People,
popularly elected, I am happy to say, by this District. Thank

you so much for your book. I have already read the Indian letters. Perhaps you are wondering what happened to my grandfather's motor cars.

PIKE: No, I hadn't really . . . What did happen to them?

RAJAH: My father presented them to the war effort. I can't think what he had in mind. Despatches carried by Rolls Royce, Staff Officers reporting for duty in snazzy Italian racing models . . . But by that time the collection had suffered the attrition of my grandfather's generosity. He gave several away, sometimes as farewell presents to his lady friends. Which brings me to your letter. To begin with, there was a disappointment. There is no Flora Crewe in the visitors book in April 1930. However, my archivist has excelled himself.

(*The* RAJAH *takes a letter from his pocket.*)

The *Collected Letters* are not complete!

PIKE: A letter from Flora?

RAJAH: A thank-you note.

PIKE: May I?

(*The* RAJAH *gives him the letter and waits while* PIKE *reads it.*)

He gave her a painting.

RAJAH: I believe we have identified it. Or rather, the volume from which it came. A miniature. From our Gita Govinda of about 1790, artist unknown. The series is by no means complete, but even so, I wish my grandfather had given her a motor-car.

PIKE: Thank you. Yes, indeed.

(*He gives the letter back.*)

RAJAH: I had a copy made for you.

(*The* RAJAH *gives* PIKE *the copy of the letter.*)

PIKE: Thank you. That was thoughtful of you. The Gita Govinda . . . would that be anything to do with a herdswoman, Radha?

RAJAH: But absolutely. It is the story of Radha and Krishna.

PIKE: Yes. And . . . erotic? She could have been nude?

RAJAH: Well, let us say, knowing His Highness, the painting would have been appropriate to the occasion.

PIKE: A watercolour, of course. On paper.

RAJAH: Are you not feeling well, Professor Pike?

PIKE: No, I'm fine. Thank you. Actually, I'm not 'Professor', I'm just one of the English Faculty . . . Please call me Eldon.

RAJAH: (*Getting up*) Well, Eldon . . . I hope I have been of some service to your biography of Miss Crewe.

PIKE: Yes. You could say that. But thanks anyway. (*Correcting*) A lot. Thanks a lot. (*Remembering himself*) Thank you, Your Highness. (*Correcting*) Sir.
(*They shake hands.*)

RAJAH: (*In Hindi*) Namaste!

PIKE: Is that your Christian name?

RAJAH: Actually, I am not Christian. No, I was saying goodbye. (*In Hindi*) Namaste!

PIKE: (*Alone; under his breath*) Oh, great.

(MRS SWAN *and* ANISH *are sitting in the garden with gin-and-tonic.* MRS SWAN *is looking at the watercolour.* ANISH *is looking at the Rajah's gift to Flora.*)

MRS SWAN: I was a shandy drinker until I went out. G-and-T takes me right back to Rawalpindi. The bottles used to say *Indian* tonic water. I was quite surprised to discover when Eric got home leave that it was Indian everywhere, and always had been. Quinine, you see. Very good for staving off malaria, though interestingly quite useless, it seemed, without the gin. Eric swore by it, the gin part, he pointed out how it got dozens of our friends through malaria until their livers gave out. Then he had a stroke on the cricket field, silly goose, umpiring without a hat.
(ANISH *and* MRS SWAN *exchange watercolours, each one being returned to its owner.*)

ANISH: From the Gita Govinda. Late eighteenth century, I think.

MRS SWAN: It was in her suitcase.

ANISH: Mine was in my father's trunk.

MRS SWAN: I didn't tell Eldon. He's not family.

ANISH: Thank you. I was in England when my father died. It was Christmas day. My first Christmas in London, in a house of student bedsits in Ladbroke Grove. An unhappy day. All the other students had gone home to their families, naturally. I was the only one left. No one had invited me.

MRS SWAN: Well, having a Hindu for Christmas can be tricky. Eric would invite his Assistant for Christmas Day lunch. It quite spoiled the business of the paper hats. There's nothing like wearing a paper hat with an Indian at table for making one feel like a complete ass.

ANISH: The telephone rang all day.

MRS SWAN: The mistletoe was another problem.

ANISH: It would stop and then start again. I ignored it. The phone was never for me. But finally I went up and answered it, and it was my uncle calling from Jummapur to say my father was dead.

MRS SWAN: Oh, and at Christmas!

ANISH: I went home. It was still 'home'. I learned that my father had left me his tin trunk which had always stood at the foot of his bed. There was nothing of value in the trunk that I could see. It was full of paper, letters, certificates, school report cards . . . (*He takes a newspaper clipping from his wallet and gives it to* MRS SWAN.) There was a newspaper cutting, however – a report of a trial of three men accused of conspiring to cause a disturbance at the Empire Day celebrations in Jummapur in 1930. My father's name was there.

MRS SWAN: (*Reading*) 'Nirad Das, aged 34.'

ANISH: That is how I know the year. His birthday was in April and Empire Day was in May.

MRS SWAN: May the 24th, Queen Victoria's birthday.

ANISH: This is how I found out. My father never told me.

MRS SWAN: And this painting?

ANISH: Yes. Underneath everything was this painting. A portrait of a woman, nude, but in a composition in the old Rajasthani style. Even more amazing, a European woman. I couldn't imagine who she was or what it meant. I kept it, of course, all these years. Then, a week ago, in the shop window . . . It was like seeing a ghost. Not her ghost; his. It was my father's hand, his work, I had grown up watching him work. I had seen a hundred original Nirad Dases, and here was his work, not once but repeated twenty times over, a special display. *The Collected Letters of Flora Crewe*, and I saw that it was the same woman.

MRS SWAN: Yes. Oh yes, it's Flora. It's as particular as an English miniature. A watercolour, isn't it?

ANISH: Watercolour and gouache.

MRS SWAN: He hasn't made *her* Indian.

ANISH: Well, she was *not* Indian.

MRS SWAN: Yes, I know, I'm not gaga, I'm only old. I mean he hasn't painted her flat. Everything else looks Indian, like enamel . . . the moon and stars done with a pastry cutter. The birds singing in the border . . . and the tree in bloom, so bright. Is it day or night? And everything on different scales. You can't tell if the painter is in the house or outside looking in.

ANISH: She is in a house within a house. The Mughals brought miniature painting from Persia, but Muslim and Hindu art are different. The Muslim artists were realists. But to us Hindus, everything is to be interpreted in the language of symbols.

MRS SWAN: And a book on the pillow, that's Flora.

ANISH: Yes. That is her. Also the flowering vine . . . look where it sheds its leaves and petals, they are falling to the ground. I think my father knew your sister was dying.

MRS SWAN: Oh . . .

ANISH: She is not posing, you see, but resting.

MRS SWAN: Resting?

ANISH: This was painted with love. The vine embraces the dark trunk of the tree.

MRS SWAN: Now really, Mr Das, sometimes a vine is only a vine. Whether she posed for him or whether it's a work of the imagination . . .

ANISH: Oh, but the symbolism –

MRS SWAN: Codswallop! Your 'house within a house', as anyone can see, is a mosquito net. And the book is Emily Eden, it was in her suitcase. Green with a brown spine. You should read the footnotes!

(MRS SWAN *and* ANISH *leave as* PIKE *enters.*)

PIKE: The book was *Up the Country* (1866). Miss Eden was accompanying her brother, the Governor-General Lord Auckland, on an official progress up country. The tour, supported by a caravan of ten thousand people, including

Auckland's French chef, lasted thirty months, and Emily wrote hundreds of letters home, happily unaware that the expedition was to set the stage for the greatest military disaster ever to befall the British under arms, the destruction of the army in Afghanistan.

(NIRAD DAS and COOMARASWAMI *are sitting on* FLORA's *verandah. It is evening, nearly dark. They have not lit the lamp. A car is heard delivering* FLORA *back to the guesthouse. Possibly the sweep of the headlights shows* DAS *and* COOMARASWAMI *rising to greet* FLORA. *She approaches the verandah, dark again, not seeing them and is startled.*)

FLORA: Oh, Mr Das!

DAS: Good evening, Miss Crewe! I'm sorry if we frightened you.

FLORA: And Mr Coomaraswami!

COOMARASWAMI: Yes, it is me, Miss Crewe.

FLORA: Good evening. What a surprise.

COOMARASWAMI: I assure you – I beg you – we have not come to presume on your hospitality –

FLORA: I wish I had some whisky to offer you, but will you come inside.

COOMARASWAMI: It will be cooler for you to remain on the verandah.

FLORA: Let me find Nazrul.

COOMARASWAMI: He is not here, evidently. But perhaps now that the mistress has returned it is permitted to light the lamp?

FLORA: Yes, of course.

COOMARASWAMI: So much more pleasant than sitting in the electric light.
    (COOMARASWAMI *lights the oil lamp.*)

COOMARASWAMI: There we are. And the moon will clear the house-tops in a few minutes . . .

FLORA: Please sit down.

COOMARASWAMI: May I take this chair?

FLORA: No, that's Mr Das's chair. And this is mine. So that leaves you with the sofa.

COOMARASWAMI: (*Sitting down*) Oh yes, very comfortable.

69

Thank you, Miss Crewe. Mr Das told me that I was
exceeding our rights of acquaintance with you in coming to
see you without proper arrangement, and even more so to lie
in wait for you like *mulaquatis*. If it is so, he is blameless.
Please direct your displeasure to me.

DAS: Miss Crewe does not understand *mulaquatis*.

COOMARASWAMI: Petitioners!

FLORA: In this house you are always friends.

COOMARASWAMI: Mr Das, what did I tell you!

FLORA: But what can I do for you?

DAS: Nothing at all! We require nothing!

FLORA: Oh . . .

COOMARASWAMI: Have you had a pleasant day, Miss Crewe?

FLORA: Extremely interesting. I have been visiting his Highness
the Rajah.

COOMARASWAMI: My goodness!

FLORA: I believe you knew that, Mr Commaraswami.

COOMARASWAMI: Oh, you have found me out!

FLORA: He showed me his cars . . . and we had an interesting
conversation, about art . . .

COOMARASWAMI: And poetry, of course.

FLORA: And politics.

COOMARASWAMI: Politics, yes. I hope, we both hope – that your
association with, that our association with, in fact – if you
thought for a moment that I personally would have
knowingly brought upon you, compromised you, by
association with –

FLORA: Stop, stop. Mr Das, I am going to ask *you*. What is the
matter?

DAS: The matter?

FLORA: I shall be absolutely furious in a moment.

DAS: Yes, yes, quite so. My friend Coomaraswami, speaking as
President of the Theosophical Society, wishes to say that if
His Highness reproached you or engaged you in any
unwelcome conversation regarding your connection with the
Society, he feels responsible, and yet at the same time wishes
you to know that –

FLORA: His Highness never mentioned the Theosophical Society.

DAS: Ah.

COOMARASWAMI: Not at all, Miss Crewe?

FLORA: Not at all.

COOMARASWAMI: Oh . . . well, jolly good!

FLORA: What has happened?

COOMARASWAMI: Ah well, it is really of no interest. I am very sorry to have mentioned it. And we must leave you, it was not right to trouble you after all. Will you come, Mr Das?

FLORA: I hope it is nothing to do with my lecture?

COOMARASWAMI: (*Getting up*) Oh no! Certainly not!

DAS: Nothing!

COOMARASWAMI: Mr Das said we should not mention the thing, and how truly he spoke. I am sorry. Goodnight, Miss Crewe –

(COOMARASWAMI *shouts towards somebody distant, in Hindi, and the explanation is an approaching jingle of harness, horse and buggy;* COOMARASWAMI *goes off stage to meet it.*)

DAS: I am coming, Mr Coomaraswami. Please wait for me a moment.

FLORA: If you expect to be my friends, you must behave like friends and not like whatever-you-called-it. Tell me what has happened.

COOMARASWAMI: (*Off stage*) Mr Das!

DAS: (*Shouts*) Please wait!

FLORA: Well?

DAS: The Theosophical Society has been suspended, you see. The order came to Mr Coomaraswami's house last night.

FLORA: But why?

DAS: Because of the disturbances in the town.

FLORA: The riot?

DAS: Yes, the riot.

FLORA: I know about it. The Hindus wanted the Moslems to close their shops. What has that to do with the Theosophical Society?

COOMARASWAMI: (*Off stage*) I am going, Mr Das!

DAS: (*Shouts*) I come now!

(*To* FLORA) It is all bosh! The Theosophical Society is bosh! His Highness the Rajah is bosh! I must leave you, Miss

Crewe. (*He hesitates.*) I think I will not be coming tomorrow. Do you mind if I fetch my painting away now?

FLORA: I think that's up to you, Mr Das. I put everything inside.

(DAS *asks permission to put on the electric light.*)

DAS: May I?

(*He starts gathering his possessions.* FLORA *turns down the oil lamp.*)

FLORA: I think I should leave tomorrow.

DAS: Tomorrow?

FLORA: I think I must. Every day seems hotter than the day before.

DAS: Yes, you are right of course.

FLORA: Mr Das, did you tell people I was ill?

DAS: What do you mean?

FLORA: That I came to India for my health?

COOMARASWAMI: (*More distant*) I cannot wait, Mr Das!

DAS: (*Shouts*) A moment!

(*To* FLORA) Why do you ask me that?

FLORA: He is leaving you behind.

(*The horse and buggy are heard departing.*)

DAS: I will walk, then.

FLORA: It seems that everyone from the Rajah to the Resident knows all about me. I told no one except you. If I want people to know things, I tell them myself, you see. I'm sorry to mention it but if there's something wrong between two friends I always think it is better to say what it is.

DAS: Oh . . . my dear Miss Crewe . . . it was known to all long before you arrived in Jummapur. Mr Chamberlain's letter said exactly why you were coming. This is how it is with us, I'm afraid. The information was not considered to be private, only something to be treated with tact.

FLORA: Oh . . .

DAS: As for the Rajah and the Resident, I am sure they knew before anybody. A letter from England to Mr Coomaraswami would certainly be opened.

FLORA: Oh . . .

(DAS *is embarrassed by her tears.*)

DAS: You must not blame yourself. Please.

FLORA: Oh, Mr Das . . . I'm so glad . . . and so sorry. How idiotic I am. Have you got a hanky?

DAS: Yes . . . certainly . . .

FLORA: Thank you. And now I have made you walk. Leave everything here.

DAS: It is not far and the moon is rising, I can manage everything without difficulty.

(*He brings the easel and his box on to the verandah and returns for the canvas.*)

FLORA: Mr Das. Don't take it. (*Pause*) If it is still a gift, I would like to keep it, just as it is.

DAS: Unfinished?

FLORA: Yes. To remind me of my friend and fellow artist Nirad Das. Your handkerchief smells faintly of . . . something nice.

DAS: The portrait is yours, if you would like it, of course. I must take it off the stretcher for you, or it will not travel easily in your luggage. Perhaps I can find a knife in the kitchen, to take out the little nails.

FLORA: There are scissors on the table.

DAS: Ah, yes. Thank you. No – I think I would damage them. May I call Nazrul?

FLORA: I thought –

DAS: Yes – Mr Coomaraswami sent him away. He is suspicious of everyone. I'm sorry.

FLORA: It doesn't matter.

(*A power cut. All the lights go out. The scene continues in moonlight.*)

Oh! The electricity again!

DAS: Yes. It is Jummapur, I'm afraid.

FLORA: Never mind.

DAS: Will we meet again?

FLORA: Perhaps, if I come back this way. I must be in Bombay by July the 10th at the latest. My ship sails on the 11th.

DAS: You may take a later ship.

FLORA: No, I cannot. My sister . . . oh, you'll be horrified, but never mind – my sister is having a baby in October.

DAS: That is joyful news.

FLORA: Oh good.

DAS: Miss Crewe . . . actually, I have brought something to show
     you which I have made . . . If we are friends again . . . I
     would like you to see it.
FLORA: Then I would like to see it.
       (DAS *takes a small watercolour out of his pocket.*)
DAS: I can light the lamp.
FLORA: There is enough light. Mr Coomaraswami was quite right
       about the moon.
       (FLORA *unwraps the paper.*)
       It's going to be a drawing, isn't it? . . . Oh!
DAS: (*Nervous, bright*) Yes!
     A good joke, is it not? A Rajput miniature, by Nirad Das!
FLORA: (*Not heeding him*) Oh . . . it's the most beautiful thing . . .
DAS: (*Brightly*) I'm so pleased you like it! A quite witty pastiche –
FLORA: (*Heeding him now*) Are you going to be Indian? Please
       don't.
DAS: (*Heeding her*) I . . . I am Indian.
FLORA: An Indian artist.
DAS: Yes.
FLORA: Yes. This one is for yourself.
DAS: Yes. You are not offended?
FLORA: No, I'm pleased. It has *rasa*.
DAS: I think so. Yes. I hope so.
FLORA: I forget its name.
DAS: (*Pause*) Shringara.
FLORA: Yes. Shringara. The *rasa* of erotic love. Whose god is
       Vishnu.
DAS: Yes.
FLORA: Whose colour is blue-black.
DAS: Shyama. Yes.
FLORA: It seemed a strange colour for love.
DAS: Krishna was often painted shyama.
FLORA: Yes. I can see that now. It's the colour he looked in the
       moonlight.
       (*They stand still, and in the moment the moonlight clouds to
       darkness.*)
FLORA: (*Recorded*)
       'Heat collects and holds as a pearl at my throat,

74

lets go and slides like a tongue-tip down a Modigliani,
spills into the delta, now in the salt-lick,
lost in the mangroves and the airless moisture,
a seed-pearl returning to the oyster –
et nos cedamus amori . . .'

(*Dawn.*
FLORA *lies inside the mosquito net. Approaching unseen,* PIKE
and DILIP *enter chanting.*)

PIKE and DILIP: 'It's no go the merrygoround, it's no go the
    rickshaw,
    All we want is a limousine and a ticket for the peepshow.
    Their knickers are made of crêpe de Chine, their shoes are
      made of python,
    Their halls are lined with tiger rugs, and their walls with heads
      of bison.'
    (*It is dawn for them, too. They have been up all night. They each
    have a bottle of beer. They are happy, not drunk.*)

PIKE and DILIP: 'It's no go the yogi-man, it's no go *Blavatsky*,
    All we want is a bank balance and a bit of skirt in a taxi!'

PIKE: (*Toasting*) Madame Blavatsky and Louis MacNeice!

DILIP: (*Toasting*) Madame Blavatsky and the Theosophical
    Society, coupled with Indian nationalism!

PIKE: Really?

DILIP: Oh yes. That's why the Jummapur branch was suppressed.
    The study of Indian religions is a very fine thing, no doubt,
    but politics is always the baby in the bathwater. Excuse me,
    I'll have a little rest.
    (DILIP *lies on the ground on his back.*)

PIKE: It's no go the records of the Theosophical Society, it's no go
    the newspaper files partitioned to ashes . . . All we want is the
    facts and to tell the truth in our fashion . . . Her knickers were
    made of crêpe-de-Chine, her poems were up in Bow Street,
    her list of friends laid end to end . . . weren't in it for the
    poetry. But it's no go the watercolour, it's no go the
    Modigliani . . . The glass is falling hour by hour, and we're
    back in the mulligatawny . . . But we will leave no Das
    unturned. He had a son. God, this country is so *big*! – Dilip –?

(DILIP *is asleep.* PIKE *shakes him.*)

Dilip! It's morning!

(DILIP *wakes refreshed.*)

DILIP: Ah yes. Would you like to come home for breakfast?

PIKE: Oh . . . Thanks!

DILIP: It's going to be hot today.

PIKE: It's hot *every* day.

DILIP: No, Eldon, you haven't been hot yet. But you're off to the hills, so you will be all right.

(*A car is heard approaching.* FLORA, *putting on her robe, gets out of bed and comes to meet* DURANCE *at the steps of the verandah.*)

FLORA: David . . .?

DURANCE: You're up!

FLORA: Up with the dawn. What on earth are *you* doing?

DURANCE: (*Approaching*) I'm afraid I came to wake you. Don't you sleep?

FLORA: Yes, I slept early and woke early.

DURANCE: I promised you a turn with the Daimler – remember?

FLORA: Yes.

DURANCE: I wanted to show you the sunrise. There's a pretty place for it only ten minutes down the road. Will you come?

FLORA: Can I go in my dressing-gown?

DURANCE: Well . . . better not.

FLORA: Right-o. I'll get dressed.

DURANCE: Good.

FLORA: Come up.

(DURANCE *comes up the verandah steps.*)

I'll be quick.

(*She goes into the bedroom. She hurriedly puts on a dress.*)

DURANCE: (*Calling from the verandah*) The damnedest thing happened to me just now.

FLORA: Can't hear you!

(DURANCE *steps closer, outside the bedroom door.*)

DURANCE: That fellow Das was on the road. I'm sure it was him.

FLORA: (*Dressing*) Well . . . why not?

DURANCE: He cut me.

FLORA: What?

DURANCE: I gave him a wave and he turned his back. I thought –
'well, that's a first!'

FLORA: Oh! There's hope for him yet.

DURANCE: They'll be throwing stones next. (*Then registering her
remark*) What?

FLORA: Come in, it's quite safe.

(DURANCE *enters the bedroom.* FLORA, *dressed, puts on her
shoes, drags a hairbrush through her hair . . .*

DURANCE *picks up Flora's book from beside the unmade bed.*)

DURANCE: Oh . . .! You're reading Emily Eden. I read it years
ago.

FLORA: We'll miss the sunrise.

DURANCE: (*With the book*) There's a bit somewhere . . . she
reminds me of you. 'Off with their heads!'

FLORA: Whose heads?

DURANCE: Hang on, I'll find it – it was Queen Victoria's
birthday . . . Oh!

FLORA: What?

DURANCE: Nothing. I found your bookmark.

FLORA: I'm ready. It's not my bookmark, I put it there for safe
keeping.

DURANCE: Where did you get such a thing?

FLORA: His Highness gave it to me.

DURANCE: Why?

FLORA: Because I ate an apricot. Because he is a Rajah. Because
he hoped I'd go to bed with him. I don't know.

DURANCE: But how could he . . . feel himself in such intimacy
with you? Had you met him before?

FLORA: No, David –

DURANCE: But my dear girl, in accepting a gift like this don't you
see – (*Pause*) Well, it's your life, of course . . .

FLORA: Shall we go?

DURANCE: . . . but I'm in a frightfully difficult position now.

FLORA: Why?

DURANCE: Did he visit you?

FLORA: I visited him.

DURANCE: I know. Did he visit you?

FLORA: Mind your own business.

DURANCE: But it is my business.

FLORA: Because you think you love me?

DURANCE: No, I . . . Keeping tabs on what His Highness is up to is one of my . . . I mean I write reports to Delhi.

FLORA: (*Amused*) Oh heavens!

DURANCE: You're a politically sensitive person, actually, coming here with an introduction from that man Chamberlain . . . I mean this sort of thing –

FLORA: Oh, darling policeman.

DURANCE: How can I ignore it?

FLORA: Don't ignore it. Report what you like. I don't mind, you see. *You* mind. But I don't. I have never minded.

(FLORA *steps on to the verandah.*)

(*In despair*) Oh – look at the sky! We're going to be too late!

DURANCE: (*To hell with it*) Come on! Our road is due west – if you know how to drive a car we'll make it.

(*They dash towards the car . . . the car doors are heard slamming, the engine roars into life and the Daimler takes off at what sounds like a dangerous speed.*)

(FLORA, *with her suitcase packed, is writing at her verandah table.*)

FLORA: 'Oh dear, guess what? You won't approve. Quite right, darling. It's definitely time to go. Love 'em and leave 'em.'

PIKE: (*Entering*) The man was most probably the Junior Political Agent at the Residency, Captain David Arthur Durance, who took F.C. dancing and horseriding. He was killed at Kohima in March 1944 when British and Indian troops halted the advance of the Japanese forces.

FLORA: 'I feel tons better, though. The juices are starting to flow again, see enclosed.'

PIKE: 'Pearl', included in *Indian Ink* (1932).

FLORA: 'I'll send you fair copies of anything I finish in case I get carried away by monsoons or tigers, and if you get a pound for them put it in the Sasha fund.'

PIKE: The reference is obscure.

(PIKE *leaves.*)

78

(MRS SWAN *and* ANISH *enter. He carries his briefcase. She has Flora's copy of Emily Eden.*)

ANISH: Mrs Swan . . . Flora's letter said, 'Guess what – you won't approve . . .' . . . and Mr Pike's footnote implies that it was the Political Agent, Captain Durance, who . . .

MRS SWAN: Mr Pike presumes too much.

ANISH: Yes! Why wouldn't you approve of Captain Durance? Surely it's more likely she meant . . .

MRS SWAN: Meant what, Mr Das?

ANISH: I don't mean any offence.

MRS SWAN: Then you must take care not to give it.

ANISH: But would you have disapproved of a British Army Officer, Mrs Swan? More than of an Indian painter?

MRS SWAN: Certainly. Mr Pike is spot-on there. In 1930 I was working for a communist newspaper. Which goes to show that people are surprising. But you know that from your father, don't you?

ANISH: Why?

MRS SWAN: He must have surprised you too. The terror of the Empire Day gymkhana, the thrower of mangoes at the Resident's Daimler.

ANISH: Yes. Yes. He must have – altered.

MRS SWAN: Yes. One alters.

(*She gives* ANISH *the book by Emily Eden.*)

This is yours. It belonged to your father. It has his name in it.

(ANISH *takes the book wordlessly and opens it.*)

I hope you're not going to blub. And you musn't make assumptions. When Flora said I wouldn't *approve*, she did not mean this man or that man. Cigarettes, whisky and men were not on the menu. She didn't need Dr Guppy to tell her that. No, I would not have approved. But Flora's weakness was always romance. To call it that.

ANISH: She had a romance with my father.

MRS SWAN: Quite possibly. Or with Captain Durance. Or His Highness the Rajah of Jummapur. Or someone else entirely. It hardly matters, looking back. Men were not really important to Flora. If they had been, they would have been

79

fewer. She used them like batteries. When things went flat, she'd put in a new one . . . I'll come to the gate with you. If you decide to tell Mr Pike about the watercolour, I'm sure Flora wouldn't mind.

ANISH: No. Thank you, but it's my father I'm thinking of. He really wouldn't want it, not even in a footnote. So we'll say nothing to Mr Pike.

MRS SWAN: Good for you. I don't tell Mr Pike everything either. It's been an unusually interesting day, thanks to you, Mr Das.

ANISH: Thank you for tea. The Victoria sponge was best! The raspberry jam too.

MRS SWAN: I still have raspberries left to pick, and the plums to come. I always loved the fruit trees at home.

ANISH: At home?

MRS SWAN: Orchards of apricot – almond – plum – I never cared for the southern fruits, mango, paw-paw and such like. But up in the North West . . . I was quite unprepared for it when I first arrived. It was early summer. There was a wind blowing. And I have never seen such blossom, it blew everywhere. There were drifts of snow-white flowers piled up against the walls of the graveyard. I had to kneel on the ground and sweep the petals off her stone to read her name.

(ANISH *has left.* MRS SWAN *remains.*)

(NELL *is bending over a gravestone . . . watched by* ERIC.)

MRS SWAN: 'Florence Edith Crewe . . . Born March 21st 1895 . . . Died June 10th 1930. *Requiescat In Pace*.'

ERIC: I'm afraid it's very simple. I hope that's all right.

NELL: Yes. It was good of you.

ERIC: Oh no, we look after our own. Of course.

NELL: I think she would have liked 'Poet' under her name. If I left some money here to pay for it . . .?

ERIC: There are funds within my discretion. You may count on it, Miss Crewe. Poet. I should have thought of that. It is how *we* remember your sister.

NELL: Really?

80

ERIC: She read one evening. The Club has a habit of asking guests to sing for their supper and Miss Crewe read to us . . . from her work.

NELL: Oh dear.

ERIC: (*Laughs gently*) Yes. Well, we're a bit behind the times, I expect. But we all liked her very much. We didn't know what to expect because we understood she was a protegee of Mr Chamberlain who had lectured in the town some years before. Perhaps you know him.

NELL: Yes. I'm not really in touch with him nowadays.

ERIC: Ah. It was just about this time of year when she was here, wasn't it? It was clear she wasn't well – these steps we just climbed, for instance, she could hardly manage them. Even so, death in India is often more unexpected, despite being more common, if you understand me. I'm talking far too much. I'm so sorry. I'll wait at the gate. Please stay as long as you wish, I have no one waiting for me.

NELL: I won't be a moment. Flora didn't like mopers.

(ERIC *leaves her.*)

(*Quietly*) Bye bye, darling . . . oh – damn!

(. . . *because she has burst into sobs. She weeps unrestrainedly.*)

ERIC: (*Returning*) Oh . . . oh, I say . . .

NELL: Oh, I'm sorry.

ERIC: No – please . . . can I . . .?

(NELL *stops crying after a few moments.*)

NELL: I've messed up your coat. I've got a hanky somewhere.

ERIC: Would you like to . . .? Here . . .

NELL: Yes. Thank you.

(*She uses his handkerchief.*)

I came too soon after all. I hated waiting a whole year but . . . well, anyway. Thank you, it's a bit wet. Should I keep it? Oh look, I've found mine, we can swap.

ERIC: Don't you worry about anything. What a shame you had to come on your own. You have another sister, I believe. Or a brother?

NELL: No. Why?

ERIC: Oh. Flora was anxious to return to England to be an *aunt*, she said.

NELL: Yes. I had a baby in October. He only lived a little while, unfortunately. There was something wrong.

ERIC: Oh. I'm so sorry.

NELL: It's why I couldn't come before.

ERIC: Yes, I see. What rotten luck. What was his name?

NELL: Sasha.

MRS SWAN: Alexander, really. Alexander Percival Crewe.

NELL: How nice of you to ask. Nobody ever does. I say, how about that blossom!

ERIC: Yes, it's quite a spot, isn't it? I hope you stay a while. First time in India?

NELL: Yes.

ERIC: Mind the loose stone here. May I . . .?

NELL: Thank you. I'm sorry I blubbed, Mr Swan.

ERIC: I won't tell anyone. Do call me Eric, by the way. Nobody calls me Mr Swan.

NELL: Eric, then.

ERIC: Do you like cricket?

NELL: (*Laughs*) Well, I don't play a *lot*.

ERIC: There's a match tomorrow.

NELL: *Here*?

ERIC: Oh yes. We're going to field a Test team next year, you know.

NELL: We?

ERIC: India.

NELL: Oh.

(*As they go,* PIKE *enters, looking for the right grave. He finds it, he takes his hat off and stands looking at it.*)

FLORA: 'Darling, that's all from Jummapur, because how I'm packed, portrait and all, and Mr Coomaraswami is coming to take me to the station. I'll post this in Jaipur as soon as I get there. I'm not going to post it here because I'm not. I feel fit as two lops this morning, and happy, too, because something good happened here which made me feel halfway better about Modi and getting back to Paris too late. That was a sin I'll carry to my grave, but perhaps my soul will stay behind as a smudge of paint on paper, as if I'd always

82

been here, like Radha who was the most beautiful of the
herdswomen, undressed for love in an empty house.'
(FLORA *puts her letter into an envelope and seals it.*
Elsewhere, NELL *kneels on the floor, going through the contents
of Flora's – duplicate – suitcase. She looks at the blue dress
briefly. She finds the rolled-up canvas. She looks at it and puts it
back.*
NAZRUL *enters to take Flora's suitcase to the train.*
FLORA *goes to the train carrying her copy of Emily Eden.*
The train makes its reappearance. COOMARASWAMI, *holding his
yellow parasol, is on the station platform to take leave of* FLORA.
He garlands her. NAZRUL *puts Flora's suitcase on the rack
above her seat.* FLORA *enters the train-compartment, gives*
NAZRUL *a tip, and bids him farewell.*
NELL *finds Flora's copy of the Emily Eden book in the suitcase.
She opens it and finds the Rajah's gift in the book. She replaces
the 'bookmark' and glances through the book.*
FLORA *waves as the train starts to depart. During the recording
of Emily Eden's letter,* FLORA *finds her place in the book, and is
reading it to herself as we hear her voice.*)
FLORA: (*Recorded*) 'Simla, Saturday, May 25th, 1839. The
Queen's Ball "came off" yesterday with great success . . .
Between the two tents there was a boarded platform for
dancing, roped and arched in with flowers . . . There was a
very old Hindu temple also prettily lit up. Vishnu, to whom I
believe it really belonged, must have been affronted. It was
the most beautiful evening; such a moon, and the mountains
looked so soft and *grave*, after all the fireworks and glare.
Twenty years ago no European had ever been here, and there
we were with a band playing, and observing that St Cloup's
Potage à la Julienne was perhaps better than his other soups,
and so on, and all this in the face of those high hills, and we
one hundred and five Europeans being surrounded by at
least three thousand Indians, who looked on at what we call
our polite amusements, and bowed to the ground if a
European came near them. I sometimes wonder they do not
cut all our heads off and say nothing more about it.'
(*The train clatters loudly and fades with the light.*)